RACIAL HEALING

RACIAL HEALING
The Institutes for the Healing of Racism

by
Reginald Newkirk
and
Nathan Rutstein

National Resource Center for the Healing of Racism
Albion, Michigan

The National Resource Center for the Healing of Racism, Albion, Michigan
Copyright © 2000 by the National Resource Center for the Healing of Racism

All rights reserved. Published 2000

Printed in the United States of America
02 01 00   3 2 1

[Cataloging-in-Publication Data]

ISBN: 0-9703864-0-0

Design by Patrick Falso, Allegro Design Inc.

CONTENTS

FOREWORD

Everyone's story counts, and everyone's story is an important part of our global history. Unlearning what we have been taught through experience or hearsay and restructuring our thoughts and beliefs are undeniable signposts on the path to freedom from racism. Writing and rewriting our personal story is a critical part of healing and requires commitment and dedication. This book represents the challenges and hopes associated with the healing process and is a guide to the Institutes for the Healing of Racism.

The Institutes for the Healing of Racism provide a safe and compassionate venue for those who are ready to eradicate the disease of racism within themselves and within our society. Through the education of the mind and the heart, participants are able to reach within themselves and begin healing. The dialogue of the spirit allows us to move deeper into ourselves and speak from our core. As we recount our stories, we begin to see the scars left by the closing of our hearts simply that we might survive. Wounded and unable or unwilling to express the pain, we walk around separated from one another and even separated from ourselves. We are unable to see that our wholeness lies in recognizing our oneness. Our very survival depends on our ability to see, hear, and recognize each other and our relationship to one another. The Institutes for the Healing of Racism bring us closer to that relationship.

In my own healing I have had to face the various aspects of myself so that the healing might be complete. The most painful part of my personal healing process was recognizing my own collusion with those who saw me as inferior and accepting the challenge of taking responsibility for my own changes. I had to face the fact that my own internalized racism had turned into a vengeance that kept my innermost talents hidden from the world. After all, why should I allow those who had oppressed me to get the best of me? Although I had convinced myself that I was doing my very best, when I began to heal I realized that I wasn't; I had so much more in reserve. The healing process has opened a reservoir of passion for my work and my relationships that I didn't know I had. Although I was always excellent at what I did, a little part of me was heavy-laden with the burden of my color and felt hopeless. In hopelessness and futility the hidden belief was "What's the point?" No matter what I did, it would never be good enough for this world. The truth of my healing began when I took my wholeness out of the hands of others and began to find it within myself.

My willingness to face my own internalized racism, which had manifested itself in the form of self-victimization and in the denial of my anger and hatred toward those who had denied me, has been a blessing for me. It has given me a sense of freedom that has allowed me to see the light of peace. Moreover, the recognition of my wholeness is allowing me to see the wholeness in others. My acknowledgment of my ability to love, to be compassionate, and to understand is changing all areas of my life.

This book is about a powerful process of healing. The process is not a quick fix. Unlearning what we have learned over many years often takes time. The parts of us that are attached and addicted to our old ways may fight the process. But once we embark on this journey, the freedom and joy that we will experience in all of our relationships is well worth the investment of time and effort.

The Institutes for the Healing of Racism allow the participants an opportunity to grow by learning from each other. The programs are presented in a non-threatening, safe environment that honors and respects all participants. As you read this text with an open mind and an open heart, it is my sincerest hope that your spirit will be touched. It is my wish that you will see yourself in the history and dedication of the two writers and that you will walk through your healing knowing that you are not alone. There are many who, like you, desire to heal. We at the National Resource Center for the Healing of Racism are here to aid and support you in this process.

—MILAGROS ALTAGRACIA PHILLIPS
Founding Executive Director
National Resource Center
for the Healing of Racism

PREFACE

The first Institute for the Healing of Racism was started in 1988. During the twelve years since then it has expanded beyond its starting point in Houston, Texas, to hundreds of communities and public and private institutions in North America and Europe. Along the way the Institutes for the Healing of Racism have undergone some refinement, often as the result of learning from our mistakes or embracing the advice of fair-minded social observers and taking to heart whatever constructive criticism was offered.

Because the Institutes maintained no central administrative body, many of the adjustments made in the refinement process have not been passed on to all of the Institutes. Also lacking was a standardized text on the philosophy, psychology, and format of the Institutes for the Healing of Racism. Now that we have established the National Resource Center for the Healing of Racism and have a refined and tested format, we are ready for such a text. Thus this book.

In Part 1 we share with the reader the writers' personal experiences with the racial healing process from African-American and White perspectives. The purpose of sharing these experiences is to demonstrate that it is indeed possible to change one's racial attitudes and behaviors.

Part 2 explores the inner workings of the Institutes for the Healing of Racism. This should help the reader become acquainted with the spirit as well as the form of the program. It is designed not only to help people set up an Institute, or to help existing Institutes sharpen their focus and execution; it is also designed to inspire those who know little or nothing about the Institutes for the Healing of Racism to become involved in the program. The Institutes' two goals and the five steps to achieving them are set forth.

We also cite the distinguishing features of the program, describing in some detail what makes it different—and, yes, more effective—than the prevailing "diversity" programs whose primary aim is to create an atmosphere of tolerance. Our program has a much higher aim. Grounded in the firm belief that racism is essentially a psychological, emotional, and spiritual disorder affecting all Americans in varying degrees, the Institutes for the Healing of Racism employ a healing approach. Because this approach emphasizes personal transformation, participants are able to heal their racism and replace it with a genuine belief in the oneness of humankind. Such an approach also helps those people of good will who are huddled in the hard shell of denial to break out of it and engage wholeheartedly in the healing process.

Part 2 also includes a description of the Institutes' "Dialogue of the Spirit" approach, which has a profound bonding effect on its participants, be they African American, White, Hispanic, Asian American, or American Indian. It shows how suspicion, fear, anger, and distrust can be replaced by understanding, love, and a tranquil, caring heart. A thorough description of the Dialogue format is provided in an appendix. The reason for the Institutes' heavy emphasis on the need for participants to internalize the principle of the oneness of humankind is also explained.

PREFACE

There is a "how to" element in the book, which provides a step-by-step description of the two-day workshop that is designed to inspire participants to continue the racial healing process. The nuts and bolts of facilitating such a workshop is given, and the administrative structure of the Institutes is described.

Part 3 describes the Institutes' national resource center, emphasizing the services it now provides as well as those that it will offer in the future. There is also an explanation of the direction in which the Institutes for the Healing of Racism are heading and a description of the organization's future goals.

ACKNOWLEDGMENTS

This book could not have been written without the courageous and tireless effort of all who have participated in the development of the Institutes for the Healing of Racism in North America and elsewhere. We have learned much from their triumphs and, yes, their failures. What stands out most is their unstinting dedication to doing their part to help heal the disease of racism in their community, often sacrificing much time and energy.

Deserving of special recognition are those who conceived of the idea of the Institutes for the Healing of Racism. Their courage and devotion to the noble cause of working to unite humankind has helped to sustain our efforts in the race-relations field. We will never forget them: Nelson Brigoni, Elisa Brown, Jackie Cone, Sharon Davis, Barbara Hacker, Zhiani Hedayati, Barbara Inihara, Roy and Shiva Lee, Andre'nea King, Freddie and Kim Polk, Mikal Rasheed, Cherry Steinwender, and Martha Ungamootoo.

We are also indebted to the heroic work of Rita Starr, whose vision helped to create the basic dialogue format used by many Institutes for the Healing of Racism.

Starr Commonwealth's embrace of the Institutes for the Healing of Racism helped to propel the Institutes into the national spotlight. The National Resource Center for the Healing of Racism never would have come into being without Starr Commonwealth's generous help. The organization's total commitment to healing the disease of racism and to fostering the oneness of humankind is an inspiration to us. Our connection to and involvement with Starr Commonwealth was an answer to a prayer. It was the one organization that lacked any ulterior motives and truly wanted to adopt the philosophy and psychology of the Institutes for the Healing of Racism. It was apparent to us that Starr Commonwealth truly wanted to free the corporation of racial prejudice and help everyone involved internalize the reality of the oneness of humankind. To witness the growth that has taken place at the institution's nine centers in Michigan and Ohio has been a great spiritual experience. It reinforces our belief that, regardless of background and upbringing, people can change for the better.

A number of individuals at Starr Commonwealth deserve special recognition. President Arlin Ness, who possesses a pioneering spirit, took on a challenge that most persons in similar executive positions would have avoided. He knew in his heart that what the Institutes for the Healing of Racism had to offer was special and could purge the effects of racism from human hearts. In a bold action, he committed a considerable sum of money to enabling all six hundred employees to participate in two-day racial healing workshops. He trumpeted the virtues of the Institutes for the Healing of Racism far and wide, becoming, in our estimation, a modern-day champion of human rights.

Starr Commonwealth's director of training, James Cunningham, not only became a tireless promoter of the Institutes, but also helped to refine and add new exercises to the process. His kind and compassionate manner is a radiant example for all.

Starr Commonwealth's chief operating officer, Martin L. Mitchell, a gentle and caring man, persuaded the management team to check out the Institutes for the Healing of Racism as a means of freeing the organization of racial prejudice. He was moved to take such action when he heard a presentation about the Institutes at a luncheon sponsored by the Kellogg Foundation.

We are obliged to acknowledge the creative and logistical efforts put forth by Christy Barrett in drafting the Institutes' workshop manual. The manual is a necessary guide to better facilitating. Christy's sweet disposition and quick mind make working with her a pleasant experience.

We never thought a chief financial officer would have such a profound effect on us, but Christopher L. Smith has changed our minds. Starr Commonwealth's "money man" participated in the two-day workshop several times. He not only became a walking encyclopedia of information about America's racial problem; he became a public advocate of the oneness of humankind. His compassion and burning desire to see true social justice instituted in his country is an inspiration to us.

If it weren't for Vice President Gary Faircloth's tireless and persistent efforts, the first international conference of the Institutes for the Healing of Racism never would have been held. But there's more to Gary than his organizational abilities. He possesses a generous spirit, and he is a healer at heart.

We view everyone at Starr Commonwealth as part of our family.

Part 1

REGINALD'S STORY

What I'm about to share would be impossible to express had I not engaged in a racial healing process. Through my Institutes for the Healing of Racism experience, I have been able to discover what was behind my anger, which had consumed me all of my adult life. I share my story with the hope that those similarly affected with anger will read it and find a way to liberation, and with the hope that those who either consciously or subconsciously contributed to my angry state of mind will not only become sympathetic but will be inspired to heal themselves of a scourge that is eroding the soul of North America.

Growing Up African American

As a preschooler in a predominantly African-American neighborhood in Brooklyn, I had no idea what the words "racism" and "racial discrimination" meant. Mine was a lower-middle-class family whose head, my grandmother, operated a hairdressing salon. We lived in a small apartment at the rear and above her shop. When I started school I tuned in to the comments my grandmother's clients made about growing up African American in the

United States. I remember thinking at the time, "Some of the stuff they're saying is scary."

Because my father didn't live with us, my immediate family consisted of my grandmother, my mother, and my two sisters. I'm the oldest of my mother's three children. My siblings and I run the gamut of color within our family. My youngest sister, Barbara, is light-skinned, while Laverne is very dark. My complexion is in between. This has never been an issue for us. We love, support, encourage, and assist one another no matter the sacrifices that may be entailed. One bit of advice from my grandmother that has helped me to survive in North America's racially hostile atmosphere is, "You can accomplish whatever you wish, as long as you put your mind to it." I must admit there were times when I doubted whether my grandmother's encouraging words would be true for me. The racial barriers were so hard to hurdle.

My mother worked two jobs: During the day she was a piece worker in New York City's garment district, and at night (after taking care of us kids) she would repair to Grandma's shop and work as a hairdresser from 7 to 11 p.m. six days a week. Sunday was church time. My grandma never took a vacation. It was work, work, work.

In our neighborhood the kids had great freedom. When I reached the fifth grade my mother permitted me to ride my bicycle to adjacent neighborhoods with my friends. We started playing sports. In those days (the early 1950s) Jackie Robinson had broken the color barrier in major league baseball. We were encouraged when we began to see the likes of Sam and K.C. Jones and Bill Russell playing on formerly all-White professional basketball teams. We were further heartened to see the first African-American football players in the National Football League on our small black-and-white television sets. Boy, did we feel proud!

But after a while my friends and I began to speculate about why so few African Americans ("Coloreds" and "Negroes" in those days) made it to the professional ranks. We saw African-American athletes on our playgrounds making tremendous moves that weren't being made by professional White athletes. We also wondered why only a handful of entertainers—people such as Sammy Davis Junior and Harry Belafonte—were featured on the Ed Sullivan Show. We were beginning to think about racial discrimination.

We went to a lot of movies. *Tarzan* was our favorite. I remember none of us ten year olds wanted to be the Africans in the films. They were depicted as savages, barbarians—ugly, brutish, and intellectually incapable of learning. I recall asking in school why Africans never made any contributions to civilization. In those days we didn't consider ourselves "Black." We were "Colored." Only the Africans were "Black." While gazing at the *Tarzan* films, I used to say to myself, "Gee, I sure am glad I'm Colored and not African." It never occurred to my friends and me that the images and stories projected on the screen were figments of the imagination of filmmakers. To us they were reality. So, too, were the films about the old South. They depicted slave life as a happy experience. The slave owners were portrayed as intelligent, God-fearing, humanitarian souls. People of such class and education could not possibly do something that would demean another human being—including slaves. Deep down I wanted what those White gentlemen and ladies had. Those same films portrayed the slaves as slow-witted, lazy, uneducable, untrustworthy, and suited only for menial tasks. It was not easy for us kids to disassociate ourselves from such "creatures." We would say to one another, "Man, that is definitely not us!" It never occurred to us that the main character in the story titled *Little Black Sambo* was not the story of a person of African descent but was about a person from India. The caricatures in the book depict an African. It was many years later that I realized tigers do not exist in Africa but rather in Asia, especially in India. These distinctions are very difficult for a child to discover alone. The elephants in the book have small ears, which indicate they are from the Indian subcontinent; African elephants have large ears. At the time I didn't know the difference. A lot of other kids and I were being brainwashed.

We used to go to the Saturday matinee and see two or three feature-length movies and at least three cartoons, plus a serial like *The Lone Ranger* or *Fu Manchu*. There were lots of cowboy-and-Indian films. I always sided with the cowboys or federal troops. I remember feeling relieved every time the cavalry charged to rescue the White settlers and cheering extra hard whenever they mauled and drove off the "bad-guys"—the Indians. All I knew about the Indians was what I saw in the movies. I couldn't understand why they stood in the way of American progress.

Cheering for the American cavalry was a part of my education. I was taught, along with many other young people of all races, that American Indians had been a barrier to American economic and social development. They were depicted as savages with little or no culture, devoid of human attributes. No one in school taught us about the contributions American Indians made in the development of humankind. Frankly my friends and I had been brainwashed to think that American Indians were less than human.

Not only was I miseducated about American Indians, but in the schools I attended in Brooklyn I learned nothing about the accomplishments of Africans in Africa or about the achievements of African Americans. What I learned from kindergarten through high school was what people of European descent had contributed to the development of Western civilization.

Even the nursery rhymes and fairy tales featured White heroes and heroines. Jack and Jill, as well as Little Bo Peep and Mary, were White. So was her little lamb.

In elementary school I grew rebellious both inside and outside of the classroom. I was becoming conscious of the fact that I was being excluded from a society in which Whites were preferred and people like me were relegated to a lower social status. I was so troublesome that my mother decided to send me to an all African-American boarding school in North Carolina for a year. At first I rebelled. The people there, not only the kids, spoke differently and had different mannerisms. They were people of the soil, and I was a big-city guy. In the beginning I called home often, mainly to hear some Brooklynese. It took about three months before I realized that my mother had done the right thing.

At this school all of the teachers and administrators were African American. Back in Brooklyn they were all White. That took some adjusting. But in the end it proved to be extremely helpful. For the first time I learned about my African heritage and about the accomplishments of African Americans. Aside from George Washington Carver and Booker T. Washington, I had not known before that there had been many African-American scientists, poets, inventors, philosophers, political leaders, and successful businessmen and women. Learning about them was part of our social studies curriculum. This information was so important that we were tested on it. We not only took academic subjects, but we were taught about nature and agriculture. Great emphasis was placed on character development. It was at this school that I not only learned the importance of service to one's community, but I actually took part in such an enterprise. Through that experience I learned the value of cooperation.

Though I looked forward to seeing my family, I felt bad when I had to leave the school at the end of the academic year.

I returned to Brooklyn with a deeper appreciation of my heritage. That gave me more confidence. I no longer viewed myself as a "Colored boy." I had a sense of being part of a race that had made some outstanding contributions to the development of humankind.

Gangs, Anger, and My Father

It was not long before I found myself under the urban spell. There was no picking butter beans in Brooklyn. I was soon ensnared by the intrigue of "hustling." To make some extra cash, my friends and I organized social parties, charging those who wanted to participate. When the reputation of our parties spread, we were swamped with paid participants. Many of my friends became so popular that they were invited to parties held by adults. It was there that many of them were introduced to cocaine, heroine, and pot. It was not long before they were strolling the avenue in flashy suits with wads of money in their pockets. They became drug pushers with a personal yen for the stuff. To many of the younger set these friends of mine, who were basically good guys, became neighborhood heroes. Tragically, many of these so-called heroes ended up going to jail or dying before they reached twenty.

Fortunately I was too chicken to try dope. Some of my clean friends and I organized a system of trying to keep those who overdosed alive. Our approach was rather basic. The first thing we would do to an overdosed friend was to slap his face several times hard. Then we would pour coffee down his throat, following that with a quart of orange juice, to which had been added half-pound of sugar. The idea was to stimulate him so much that he would stay awake. If he fell asleep he would die.

Even today I feel uneasy among the police. It doesn't matter if they are in a good mood. It is something that's been inbred in me, and I will probably never get rid of it.

In Brooklyn many of my friends and I had some serious encounters with the cops. We didn't respect or trust them, and we had reason to feel that way. Some officers treated us badly. We would often be stopped and searched without provocation, especially if we were gathered together on the corner or walking down the street. They were looking for drugs and weapons. Our answers to their questions were often met with skepticism and, at times, derision or worse.

We didn't trust the police because they tried to plant drugs on us. One time while we were walking to the community center to attend a dance, a patrol car pulled up, and two officers stepped out and told us to stop in our tracks. They immediately told us to "assume the position," which meant facing the building with our legs spread and our arms plastered against the wall. After searching us they grilled us for about twenty minutes, asking where we lived, what school we attended, whether we had any drugs or weapons. We responded honestly. After a lecture on staying out of trouble, the policemen took off. Our immediate response was to search our pockets. I found nothing, but one of my friends who never smoked marijuana found in his pocket a partially smoked joint. He had almost become another victim of a police plant job. He dispensed with the roach by dropping it into the sewer.

A few minutes later those same cops caught up with us, and of course ordered us to "assume the position" again. After searching us thoroughly they seemed a bit bewildered. They had not found what they thought they would find. After enduring some verbal harassment, we were allowed to go our way.

My friends and I were angry as hell, and not merely because of the way the police treated us. We were angry about the lynchings, the racial discrimination we read about in the South. We were angry with our schools, which put us down as young African-American men. We could tell that most of our teachers thought we were not as smart as White kids. We were angry with our families for not fighting back, for allowing us to be treated as less than equals.

There wasn't much we could do about what was happening in the South, but there was something we could do in our neighborhood to get back at those who mistreated us, humiliated us, or belittled us because of our skin color. We would rationalize our unlawful acts directed against our enemies by convincing ourselves that they deserved whatever they got. We paid back the schools by vandalizing them, stealing whatever we could get our hands on, and intimidating our teachers. Our teenage vengeance provided us with some emotional relief.

While I was eternally grateful to my mother, my grandmother, and my favorite aunt, Ethel, for all their guidance, love, and kindness, what they said to me during my teens did not mean as much, at the time, as the advice I received from my fellow gang members. I was somebody in the gang. At home I was simply "Reggie." In the gang I had a reputation that commanded respect from my fellow gang members as well as from members of other gangs. I became the warlord of my gang because I could punch people out a lot better than others could. Being in the gang gave me some power and respect in the community, even among some adults. In our world the gang had its rules, its pecking order, and its support network. We gave counsel to each other. We offered consolation to one another in times of difficulty. We stood up for one another. We were, in an odd sense, a united family. The older guys in our gang acted as big brothers to us younger guys, giving to me, at times, fatherly advice.

Not having my father around most of the time while growing up was hurtful. Perhaps that was one of the reasons I joined the gang. As a kid I was disappointed so many times by him that I would turn numb whenever he would show up. Looking back, I realize my attitude toward him was an act of self preservation, but as an adult I have moved beyond resenting my father. Though living in Canada with a wife and three children, I would continually visit my mother and sisters on a regular basis. On one of our visits my sisters arranged for my father to meet me and my family. When he arrived I was seized by a strange feeling: I wanted to belt him and hug him at the same time. But I controlled myself. I immediately introduced him to his grandchildren. It didn't take long before my father decided he wanted to take me and my eldest son, Tallis, for a haircut at his favorite barbershop.

My father, with an obvious sense of pride, introduced me to his barbershop buddies. Then, with an even greater measure of pride and sheer delight, he introduced his grandson to the men. He began to talk about how bright and intelligent his grandson was. Of course, at the same time, my father made it clear that such abilities had emerged from his gene pool! I was puzzled, confused, resentful, and hurt as I witnessed such an effusion of loving care, kindness, and pride pour out of my father's heart. As I watched, I thought, I wish he would have showered that kind of affection toward me. But he never did.

I was living in Nova Scotia when I received news of my father's death. I made immediate plans to attend the funeral, unaware of the surprise that awaited me. After the funeral service, some of my relatives introduced me to two half-brothers and two half-sisters who were children of my father.

To learn in my forty-fourth year of life that I had four other siblings who had not been part of my life was an astounding discovery. We spent hours together discussing our father. I am the oldest and had the least contact with him.

Before I learned of my father's passing I had been working on a letter to send to him. It was one of the toughest tasks of my life. I wanted to say certain things to him that I couldn't say in his presence. Completing the letter was a lot easier after I received news of his death, but I wish he had been alive to read it. In a way I felt cheated that he wasn't around to hear how I really felt about him. So I did the next best thing: I took the letter to his graveside. When my relatives returned to their cars, I remained, peering down on my father's casket. Before reading the letter, I recited a beautiful prayer for the deceased. Then, with my heart racing, I proceeded to talk aloud. I told him that I had been working for weeks on a letter, that I had many things to tell him, and that I wished he were alive to hear what was festering in my heart. But I said that he would not completely escape from hearing what I needed to tell him. Before the cemetery attendants began shoveling the soil over the coffin, I took out the letter from my pocket, and with a deep sigh and mustering up my courage, I began to read the letter, oblivious of anyone around me. I told him about my heartbreak when he had not been around for my high school graduation or for my track meets and basketball games. Seeing my friends' dads there had made it even more painful. I told him how it was difficult for me to truly understand what it means to be a man and a father because I had not had a direct role model in my life because he simply had not been there. I told him how angry that made me, how I have had to struggle with that anger in all my relationships—with my wife, children, relatives, friends, work, and business associates.

I kept on reading, ignoring the pleas of my relatives to return to the car. I had to finish what I had to do. Tears poured down my cheeks as I read on. I knelt at his grave and recited a prayer for the progress of his soul. A wave of compassion swept over me, and I cried out, "I forgive you, Dad!" Then I asked his forgiveness for whatever disappointment I might have caused him in his life. I stood up and tossed the letter onto my father's coffin, declaring, "Dad, here is my letter. Don't think that you are going to leave this life without it." I stood in silence for a few minutes while attendants started to fill in the plot. I finally left with a feeling of relief. The graveside experience had lifted a burden I had carried within my heart for so long.

Back in Brooklyn I began to recall more of my gang experiences. There were lots of battles with other gangs, some of them bloody, and they weren't always with Whites. Perhaps our bloodiest battles were with other African Americans from different neighborhoods. In one of the scariest battles, we were outnumbered, maybe two to one. The other gang had many more weapons—homemade pistols, swords, bayonets, knives, and chains. When the opposing gang surrounded us, one of our guys moved toward one of the enemy and stabbed the guy in the shoulder. That produced an opening in the ring, and most of us dashed through it. The other gang was in hot pursuit. As we ran down a main street that led to a subway station, we encountered a number of police officers and pleaded with them to keep those who were pursuing us from harming us. When the cops saw how many of the other gang members were chasing us, they fled too. I bolted down into the subway station, jumped the turnstile, and caught a waiting train along with some of my friends. A member of the other gang made the mistake of hopping onto the same train.

It didn't take long before fifteen members of my gang pounced on the kid and began beating him to a pulp. The beating was sickening. There was no honor in fifteen guys pounding one guy. I left the car in disgust and moved into a car at the front of the train. A few minutes later the guy who had been the target of my friends' wrath stumbled into the car I was in. He was holding his neck. I could see blood spurting from it. It seemed to me that an artery had been cut. I went over to him, unsure of what I could do to help him. But something had to be done because I knew that if the bleeding wasn't stopped, he would die. After guiding the guy to the floor, I took off my new trench coat and tied it around his neck. I knotted the coat sleeves at the point on his neck from which the blood was flowing. About five minutes later the train stopped at a station. In came what seemed to be a regiment of cops. I had never seen so many police gathered at once for anything other than a parade. They were arresting every African-American male in sight. When they came to arrest me, an elderly white woman who had witnessed what I had done for that unfortunate kid convinced the cops to leave me alone, explaining what I had done for the guy. Watching that woman come to my defense, I turned to God and uttered a prayer of thanksgiving, "Oh, thank you Lord for this dear old lady's help."

That day I thought I would never go rumbling with my gang again. But that feeling was short-lived. Within two weeks I was at it again. As the warlord of the Seventh Division of the Corsair Lords, it was my job to fight my counterpart in an opposing gang. Usually such encounters determined whether the gangs would wage war.

Deep down I wanted to quit the gang. I was tired of the senseless fighting. I knew it wasn't the right thing to do. But there was pressure from my friends to stay the course. When guys who have been your buddies ever since you started to walk try to make you believe that you are irreplaceable, it is tough to say "No."

Most of our gang rumbles were with other African-American gangs. The fights were usually over turf and maintaining our tough-guy reputation. I recall some battles with White and Hispanic gangs. They often broke out when someone uttered a racial slur; after classes the school yard would become a battlefield. The teachers didn't dare to pull us apart.

There were a few White guys whom we trusted and got close to. In fact, several of them joined our singing group. We had a pretty good gig going. Singing in the subway stations was our stage, and it was a good place to make lunch money. We liked singing there because of the echo chamber effect. It made our harmony sound much fuller, more soothing. It was a creatively fulfilling experience with White guys who, after a while, weren't considered White anymore to the African-American guys in the troupe.

Are We as Good as They Are?

As a child and youth I would hear African-American adults at picnics and parties talking about not trusting African-American professionals such as doctors, dentists, and lawyers. "If you can go to a White professional, do it," they would say. The message I got from that recommendation was that African-American professionals weren't as smart or as skilled as the White ones, and I believed it. So when I was only five years old my grandmother took me to an African-American physician. I was scared as hell. This man is going to harm me, I thought. I was looking for television's Dr. Kildare, who was White, to come to my rescue. Because the adults never included scientists in their list of African-American professionals to avoid, I decided to become a scientist.

As I grew older, I heard African-American men and women saying in the streets and even in stores, "Niggers ain't shit." In my mind, that statement was linked to the views I had heard about African-American professionals. I noticed something else that puzzled me, a phenomenon that still exists. If an African-American person accomplished something the rest of us on my block did not achieve, in some inexplicable way, we seemed to feel diminished by it. Jealousy abounded. Someone who seemed to make it in the White man's world was viewed as "uppity." This was especially true when it came to education. Those of us who tried to do well in school were accused of trying to "act White." It was very confusing to me, because we were trying to better our lot in life, yet if we dared to make strides in that direction we were criticized and stigmatized.

When I was in the ninth grade I came across a saying that seemed to perpetuate the social condition in our neighborhood and in other predominantly African-American neighborhoods: "If you white, you all right; if you brown, stick around; but if you black, get back, way back." Such self-deprecating remarks are an indication of internalized racism, which continues to plague the African-American community. Just as there is denial among White folks, there's plenty of denial along a wide spectrum of African Americans.

I remember the impact of the stories African-American war veterans told about their experiences on the battlefield in World War II and in the Korean conflict. They used to say things like, "Man, when I was overseas fighting to preserve American democracy we had to fight on two fronts. One was the general enemy of America, the other was making sure White officers or enlisted men did not blow me away." I remember one evening overhearing a veteran who was close to my family telling them of his experiences while serving in Europe during World War II. Before joining the troops in the war zone, his regiment was sent to England to be prepped for service on the front lines. (African Americans in those days were deemed incapable because of their race, unfit to engage in combative roles such as infantryman, tanker, artilleryman. The high command relegated African-

American troops to service roles such as cook, truck driver, laborer.) While in London on pass, he and his buddies found many of the Londoners staring at them, as if they were oddities of some sort. Wondering why this was happening, one of the guys stopped a group of Englishmen and inquired why they and so many others were looking at them in such a strange manner. One of the Englishmen said sincerely and straightforwardly, "We are looking for a sign of the tails White American soldiers told us Black soldiers have and wrap around their waist to hide." Somewhat taken aback, the African-American soldiers lifted their shirts to show that there were no tails wrapped around their waists. I was ten years old when I heard this story. I listened in rapt astonishment. I wondered why anyone would even say such a thing about other human beings. What awful things had African Americans done to White folks to cause them to tell such tales on us? I puzzled over the ignorance of such a comment. It led me to wonder, if many White people had strange ideas about African Americans, what did they think about other people such as the American Indians, Hispanics, Jews, and Asians? My imagination was not active enough to come up with any explanation for such behavior. I was confused, bewildered, and angry, and I wanted answers to questions a lot of folks were afraid to bring up.

As a child I loved reading *Ebony* and *Jet* magazines. Reading about African-American men and women accomplishing great things and being able to realize the American dream inspired me to make that dream come true for myself. My goal was to become a scientist and one day be featured in those magazines. So I studied hard and did well in all of my subjects except math. I had been told I wasn't good at math. Evidently that observation had made quite an impression on me. No amount of study was able to break that spell. When I sought help from my teachers, they rejected my pleas, reinforcing my belief that I was hopelessly dumb in math.

I ended up in the general track in high school, which wasn't designed to prepare students for college. Because the courses were easy, I was making A's and B's without much effort. It seemed that I was destined for some kind of menial job. At least that's the impression I got from my teachers and guidance counselor. But I didn't join the garbage men's union. War was raging in Vietnam. To avoid being drafted into the infantry, I joined the Air Force.

Basic training at Lackland Air Force Base was generally the same for every recruit, except for us African Americans. There were the usual slights by the drill instructors, but they were nothing new to us. We simply had to thicken our already thick, street-hardened, street-wise skin. What helped me to get through basic training without lashing out at my tormentors was focusing on the new anthem that was sweeping across the African-American community. And that was "Black is beautiful." My racial pride subdued my anger.

I was shipped to Lowery Air Force Base, where I was trained to be an air policeman specializing in combat defense force security. My unit's objective was to guard Titan One missile sites, a sensitive assignment during the Cold War. Having received such a responsible position, I felt the Air Force believed I had some worth. Maybe, I thought, I should shoot for a career in the military. Why not try to become an officer? I said to myself. So I took a battery of tests to see if I would qualify to enter the Officers Training Program.

When I learned I had failed the tests, that feeling of being a dummy, which had been drilled into me at school, was intensified. I was now convinced that I was not smart. To this day I carry some doubt about my mental abilities.

But the Air Force testing saga wasn't over. Evidently other African-American and Hispanic airmen had failed the tests also. Through the intervention of an Irish-American sergeant who felt I was officer material, it was discovered that the psychometrician who was evaluating the tests was a White supremacist. The man was failing every non-White airman who was testing for a position in the Officers Training Program. So the sergeant had a psychometrician on another military base evaluate my test, and I passed even the math section.

But by that time I had become jaded about being in the military, and I channeled my energies into the civil rights effort, which was in its heyday. While based in Colorado in the early and mid 1960s, I wanted to be involved in what was going on in the deep South at the time. A number of African-American airmen and I wanted to spend some of our furlough time participating in freedom marches in Alabama and Mississippi. But we never got to. Our wing commander told us that the Secretary of the Air Force had issued an executive order prohibiting our participation in civil rights marches and demonstrations. Disobeying the order, he said, would lead to a court marshal, which could result in jail time and a dishonorable discharge. Though we never joined the effort in the South, we worked for equal rights for minorities in the Rocky Mountain region.

It was a time of great passion. I was attracted to the rhetoric of Stokely Carmichael, who was president of the Student Nonviolent Coordinating Committee. His rationale for the "Black is beautiful" concept made a lot of sense. I dropped the words "Colored" and "Negro" from my vocabulary. I became a proud and angry Black man. Whenever I would hear the singer James Brown sing his song "I'm Black and I'm Proud," I would get goose bumps. For me the song became a personal anthem.

In the 60s and 70s I was deeply involved in straightening out my identity as a human being. To do that I became a voracious reader of anything that would clarify my heritage roots. I dug into African history and worked hard at expunging from my heart and mind all of the "White" propaganda regarding the nature of the African-American man. I found the former exciting and soul-thrilling, but the latter was a painful struggle. It isn't easy to undo what has been a part of you for decades.

I was discharged from the Air Force in June 1965 at the height of the civil rights struggle. With my experience as an air policeman, I thought I had a good chance of hooking up with the Denver police department. My application wasn't even filed in the potential candidates file. Every other attempt to gain employment was met with rejection.

I moved on to Sparks, Nevada, where I became involved as a volunteer tutoring American Indian children in the Sparks-Reno Indian Colony. Though this service project only lasted for the summer, it was an exciting experience for two reasons: I was able help a very appreciative group of youngsters improve their school work, including their math, and I discovered that I had the makings of a darn good teacher. After that summer, it was back to searching for work—anything that would keep me from becoming another homeless statistic. I tried the casinos. Since many of them were advertising that they were hiring, I thought I could get a job in one of them. It didn't matter what kind of work was available. None of them hired me, and it became clear why during one hiring session. In one hiring line the two Whites ahead of me and the two behind me got jobs, while I was told there were no more vacancies.

I was full of rage. I became somewhat disoriented. It made no sense to me to be refused a job simply because of the color of my skin or to be refused an apartment because the landlord preferred a tenant of European descent. All of this fueled my sense of indignation and outrage. I felt particularly stung by the discrimination when I thought about the fact that I could have been sent to fight in Vietnam—only to return to America (if I were so lucky) to be refused a job and denied housing because I was an African-American man.

Feelings of futility began to well up in my soul. It seemed like racism in America was undefeatable. There did not appear to be enough good will amongst the majority of White people to make a difference. I felt then, and continue to feel to this day, that American Indians, Hispanics, Asian Americans and African Americans working for the elimination of racism will not achieve much beyond the passage of laws. While anti-discrimination laws are important, they are not enough to bring about a change in the White person's heart. Any employer, landlord, or service provider who wants to discriminate against any other person will find creative ways to hire who they want, rent to whom they desire, and serve those whose patronage they seek. Notwithstanding the passage of historic civil rights legislation, there was nothing I could do to become the type of person most Whites would employ, rent to, or serve.

I prayed that I would not become one of those desperate, despairing African-American men hanging out on the street corner looking for cheap ways to dull the pain. But evidently the answer to my prayers was that I was going to be tested. At first I failed the test. Needing relief from being an African-American man in racist America, I turned to something as a child and youth I had vowed I would never indulge in: alcohol and pot. I found parties where there was lots of that stuff. I lived for the weekends, when I could escape. To my surprise, I discovered that spiritual values and high-minded social principles were insufficient to relieve my anguish. My personal sense of insecurity and lack of confidence, woven into my soul early in life, constantly tugged at both my heart and my mind. I felt the heat of rage well up in my heart whenever I thought honestly about my social and emotional condition. "This shouldn't be," I would often cry out while alone in my room. In such moments I became so angry I did not care what I did or what would happen to me. I felt as though my life was "not shit," that is, I would not be permitted to amount to anything. All the cards were seemingly stacked against me. If misery loves company, then the only solace I had was that most African-American brothers and sisters were similarly situated. But any consolation that may have been derived from such company was fleeting.

I believe meeting Tom and Marion West at a Bahá'í gathering was an answer to my prayers. Evidently God knew I could not bear any more tests. This White couple treated me as if I were their son. At first it was a bit strange, for I had never lived in a White home before. But that feeling soon vanished. Being exposed to unqualified love every moment I was in their presence purged my heart of every drop of suspicion that had been festering there for years. Tom became the father I never really had. He was an incredible role model. Like me, he was looking for a job. He had been fired because of his extracurricular activities. He was an outspoken, fearless fighter for social justice. His consistent clamoring for Nevada to free the workplace of racial discrimination had turned him into a "troublemaker" in the eyes of most employers. In time, however, he did land a job, but he never wavered in his mission to break down the racial barriers in his state. What impressed me most about Tom was that he never uttered an unkind word about anyone, even those who disliked him. Throughout the time he was unemployed he never felt sorry for himself, never expressed any bitterness; he continued to exude love toward everyone he met. This, I thought, is an example of how a true man is expected to live life. I found myself naturally trying to be like Tom, who was a long-time member of the Bahá'í Faith.

At Tom's and Marion's urging I decided to sign up for a new training program. My first reaction had been to not to do so. Deep down I felt I was incapable of succeeding. My unpleasant school experiences were haunting me. But my surrogate parents' gentle yet firm insistence that I give it a try drew me into the program. I'm glad I followed their advice, because I not only completed the six-week program and became a certified operating room technician, I quickly got a job at a Reno hospital assisting surgeons in surgery. There was a lot to know—for example, all of the aseptic techniques, the names and uses of all of the surgical instruments. It didn't take long before I grew comfortable in the operating room and, depending on the type of operation, was able to anticipate what instruments the surgeon wanted. It felt good, because my first real job after being honorably discharged from the Air Force was not hauling garbage or sweeping floors. There were times while prepping for surgery when I would think about my grandmother and mother: How they would love to see me in surgical gown, cap, and mask.

That experience not only gave me a much-needed boost in confidence, it helped to develop in me a deep appreciation for discipline and order. I was also able to save some money, and I began thinking of going to college.

While reflecting on my operating room technician training, it dawned on me that I had not experienced one racial slight. Though I had been the only African-American student, I had been evaluated on the same basis as every other student. This experience was very important to me because it showed me that it is possible to be involved in a prejudice-free White-dominated activity.

Nevertheless, I remained guarded. My struggle to achieve an inherent sense of equality had become more focused, even though the goal became elusive. I was now striving to define myself as a man of African descent living in North America. I realized that the odyssey of being and living as a person of African descent as developed in Ralph Ellison's *Invisible Man* was intimately connected with my own conscious struggle for identity. Writing on this subject in his superb work, *Trouble in Mind,* professor Leon F. Litwack summarizes the plight of the African Americans to define ourselves:

> Even as the ambitious hero [of *Invisible Man*] attends college, even as he is encouraged to believe he is making remarkable progress, even as he embraces the white man's work ethic and success credo, even as he accommodates himself to the white man's ways of thinking and acting, he finds his expectations betrayed and his goals unreachable. . . . But with every step, he must again perform the rituals expected of him, and play the role defined by whites, all of them equally dehumanizing, equally degrading, equally unrewarding.

Becoming a College Student

Having taken mostly commercial courses such as bookkeeping and typing, I couldn't be admitted into a degree-offering program at the University of Nevada-Reno. But I could take courses. I did well in the history course I took. That provided another boost in confidence. When a friend who was also a war veteran told me that he was heading for the University of Wyoming because the school was looking for nontraditional students—mature men and women—I decided to apply to that university.

You can imagine how happy I was when I received my letter of acceptance. But moments later I began to worry about whether I would succeed there. In the fall of 1966 the University of Wyoming was dominated by fraternities and sororities. None of them welcomed African Americans. Reserve Officers' Training Corps (ROTC) was big on campus, but I had had my fill with the military. Intercollegiate and intramural sports were also popular, but I was too small for football, too short for basketball, and too busy trying to learn good study habits to try out for the track team. So I buried myself in my studies, especially the sciences. I was bent on succeeding.

I ran into obstacles in my first semester. Because I wanted to be a biochemistry major, I had to take calculus. I had a poor academic background in math; in high school I had not taken algebra, geometry, or trigonometry. I found myself way over my head. The fact that I had developed a complex about math didn't help. In dropping math, I could not pursue my goal of being a scientist.

I turned to history and philosophy. African-American history especially fascinated me, mainly because it was a way of acquainting myself with my roots. Philosophy came naturally to me. Ever since I had been a kid I had engaged in conversations with a wide assortment of street philosophers in Brooklyn. Some of these men and women had wisdom you can't gain on a college campus.

Fortunately I was able to develop a major that combined history and philosophy. It was called "the history of ideas." I was also fortunate in developing friendships with five White guys who were also veterans. All of them were in the honors program and had mastered the way to study. I simply followed their example. In time I learned the nuts and bolts of studying, which led to a love for research. Unearthing evidence and appraising it was like solving a mystery. I will be eternally grateful to those five guys, and not only for helping me to organize my academic duties. I enjoyed our friendship, and the fact that I could simply be myself and did not have to pretend in their presence was a great relief. The topic of race rarely came up in our conversations. We were just friends. Not Black or White friends, simply friends.

I was challenged while at the University of Wyoming. Not academically—I could handle my major. But socially I was caught in conflict. The civil rights movement was in full swing. I wanted to be a part of it. I did the next best thing: I joined the anti-Vietnam-war effort on campus, not because I was philosophically opposed to the war, but because these were people who were opposed to racism and prejudice manifested in any form. Some of us supported the Black Panthers; others aligned themselves with the Weathermen, the militant arm of the Students for a Democratic Society. There were those who advocated the philosophy of the Student Nonviolent Coordinating Committee; some pushed the philosophy of the Urban League or the National Association for the Advancement of Colored People. Actually the philosophy that had the greatest appeal to me was that of the Bahá'í Faith, which wasn't part of the campus antiwar movement— not that the religion condoned what was going on in Vietnam.

I felt emotionally and intellectually pulled in several directions. I liked what the Black Panthers were doing to promote Black awareness and Black pride and protection of the community. The fact that they were taking a proactive role in protecting the African-American community impressed me. Their actions appealed to the warrior spirit within me. A competing pull came from the profound spiritual and social teachings of the Bahá'í Faith. Its commitment to walking the spiritual path with practical feet had an enormous impact on me. It was so balanced. To include all human beings in the struggle to transform society and eliminate prejudice and discrimination in the world is the incontrovertible goal of Bahá'ís everywhere.

It was difficult for me to sort out feelings such as loyalty to my people (African Americans) and community, to the American ideal in which I had been indoctrinated throughout high school, or to the struggle to define myself as a human being of African descent. Somehow I had to reconstruct myself, free myself from the legacy and limitations of prescriptive racial stereotypes and attitudes. There were questions that haunted me: Was I too arrogant? Too angry? Was my anger a cover up of feelings of inferiority and insecurity? Was I afraid to find out and deal with my true self?

Off to Canada

While I was in Brooklyn and even while I was in the Air Force, I had never dreamed that I would one day be living in Canada. Well, that's where I live now. What drew me to Canada was a young woman I met at a Bahá'í youth conference. She lived in Lethbridge, Alberta, a university town that also serves the needs of the surrounding wheat and sugar-beet farmers. This Brooklyn-bred dude followed her there. It didn't take long before we decided to get married. But to stay there, I needed a job, and before I could get a job I needed a work visa. My initial attempt to get the visa was turned down by an unsympathetic immigration officer.

Once again I felt trapped—this time by government bureaucracy. Was the color of my skin a factor in being turned down? I wondered. It is a question I usually ask myself whenever I'm faced with adversity.

Cindy, my wife-to-be, was comforting and felt confident that things would work out. A few days after my encounter with the immigration people, we were invited to a dinner party with one of her mother's friends. We had a wonderful time. Not only that, meeting the host, Mr. M., turned out to be a blessing. During the course of the evening, he asked what Cindy and I were going to do. We told him about our wedding plans and our hope that I would be permitted to work while attending college. He asked if I had gone to the immigration office and talked with the staff. When I told him about my experience at the office, he suggested I try again.

I followed his advice and was greeted warmly by a different immigration officer. When I mentioned my name, he replied, "Oh, yes, Mr. Newkirk, I have your papers right here. Would you please read these forms, fill in the blanks as they relate to you, and sign the forms when you have finished answering the questions." The officer then took the completed application and provided me with a temporary work visa. At the same time, he processed my application for landed immigrant status. I was stunned by the way I was treated. What could cause such a reversal of treatment and attitude? I asked myself. With temporary documents in hand, I began to make my way down the hall to a room where I was to confer with another officer. As I passed the office of the district superintendent, I took a quick look in, and there was Mr. M., sitting behind his desk, checking over some papers. After my interview I dashed to my fiancé's parents' home, where I was living, to tell the family what had happened. I asked Cindy and her parents if they were aware that Mr. M. headed the regional immigration office. They had had no idea that their friend held such an important position.

With a work permit I had no trouble landing a job as an operating room technician at a local hospital. To make some extra money, I doubled as an orderly when requested. Cindy worked as a waitress at a large hotel frequented by tourists.

When September arrived we were married. There was no big-time honeymoon because we had to start classes at the university. Since it was a relatively small college, we had access to all of our professors on and off the campus. I majored in history and philosophy and minored in anthropology. It didn't take long before I found myself involved in campus politics. I was elected the student council's vice president for external affairs. In a way, I was an oddity, for there were only five African Americans living in

Lethbridge. As far as I know I was the only person of African descent on campus.

Though I had moved to another country, I hadn't left my deep-seated sense of inferiority at the border. I couldn't shed what had been ingrained in me during my school experience in Brooklyn. Deep down I felt I was not as capable as others. Of course, over the intervening years I had found ways to mask that feeling. Creating a super-cool guy image seemed to be most effective. But there were times when even that device failed me. For example, when I received an A-minus on a paper I had written for my philosophy of education course, I thought the professor was engaged in some sort of affirmative action program. I challenged him to prove to me that I had earned the grade, that he viewed me as an equal to my peers. He assured me that I had earned the grade fair and square, pointing out that he had been impressed with the philosophical resolution to the problems set forth in the paper. That bit of reassurance helped.

I quickly learned that a college education is no antidote to racial prejudice. This notion was reinforced when my wife and I volunteered to make a presentation on interracial marriage to our anthropology class. During the question-and-answer period, a bright middle-aged, white-haired female student offered the following observation, which made me wonder about the other students' views: "As far as Canadian society is concerned, you [referring to my wife] have given up status, and he [referring to me] has gained status." I found her remark quite curious. Although she attributed the statement to society at large, I sensed that it was her personal conviction as well.

Graduation day was something special for me. I wish my teachers in Brooklyn could have been there. They would have realized that their assessment of my intellectual capacity was wrong. My graduating class elected me valedictorian, and I graduated magna cum laude, receiving a bachelor of arts degree in history and philosophy. I had earned a 3.8 grade point average out of a possible 4.0.

I thought I should have no trouble getting a job as a high school teacher, assuming that recruiters placed heavy emphasis on the candidates' college records. As far as I know, all one hundred of the school of education graduates had no trouble landing teaching jobs. However, I, the valedictorian of our class, did not land a job. And it wasn't a matter of not trying. I applied for fifty teaching positions in Alberta alone, receiving only one invitation for an interview.

I'll never forget that interview, which took place in a restaurant, with the superintendent of schools in a rural area. The man seemed gentle, very forthcoming. When he said, "I have a sensitive question to ask you," I knew I was in trouble. And when he added that I didn't have to answer the question, I knew I was in deep trouble. Mustering every ounce of bravado I could, I pretended I had no worries. I encouraged him to ask the question. After clearing his throat, he said, "I have been told that you are married to a White woman. Is that correct?" I told him that he had heard correctly. He calmly responded by assuring me that he personally had no objection to interracial marriages but that the residents in his town were not ready for it. And because of that he could not hire me. When I pointed out that his position was in violation of the provincial Human Rights Act, he refused to break with tradition and expressed an inability to change his mind.

Once again I was pressed by both historical and personal circumstances to take any job that would allow me to support my family. A good friend told me he was leaving his position to take up with the Alberta Human

Rights Branch. He suggested that I consider applying for the position he was vacating. I'm glad I applied. The idea of working with native people intrigued me. The interview with the Board of Directors of the Napi (Peigan First Nation) Friends Association went well. I was hired as the Executive Director of the Association.

At that time the Napi Friendship Association was focused on assisting Canadian Indians moving from Peigan and Kanai reservations to Pincher Creek and Fort McLeod, Alberta. The Association offered many educational, social, and sports programs. My one-and-a-half-year stay in the position was extremely rewarding. I grew to really appreciate the suffering these people have had to endure for nearly four hundred years. I was convinced that they had been the target of racism by a government that looked upon them as inherently inferior beings. In the short time I stayed at that job I made many close friendships, and I'm proud that the Association's membership elected me to both the provincial and national associations of Indian friendship centers.

With a growing family, I took an offer that paid more money. I became a Human Rights Officer with the Alberta Human Rights Branch. In that job I assessed, investigated, and conciliated complaints of discrimination made by individuals. Specifically my responsibilities involved enforcement of anti-discrimination provisions of the Alberta Human Rights Act in such areas as services and employment on the basis of race, religion, and age.

Evidently the leadership of Canada's human rights community was impressed with my work, for during a fifteen-year-period I kept receiving promotions. Canada's Human Rights Commission made me its western regional director, which initially included coverage of British Columbia, Alberta, and the Northwest and Yukon Territories.

About ten years later, while working as executive director of the Yukon

Human Rights Commission, I heard about the racial friction in Nova Scotia. There had been many newspaper and television reports highlighting the bloody fighting between African Americans and Whites. Being African American, I wanted to be there. I wanted to try my hand in helping to build bridges of understanding between the two groups. I was aware of the long-standing animosity between them. Most of the African Americans' ancestors had been pre-Civil War slaves who found refuge in Nova Scotia, never really integrating into the dominant White culture.

I felt that my prayers had been answered when I was approached at a national conference by the executive director of Nova Scotia's Human Rights Commission. Aware of my background in conflict resolution and dealing with sensitive racial situations, he wondered if I would consider coming to Nova Scotia to help the commission deal with the problem. I took the job as the commission's race relations coordinator and plunged into my work with considerable enthusiasm. Our first task was to design and test a training program. Next we trained forty people as workshop facilitators. These facilitators would have the responsibility of facilitating two-day workshops for the ten thousand civil-service workers in the province. The idea was to help the participants develop a more compassionate attitude in their encounters with people of different races. Though we completed the task and most of the participants found the experience useful, I'm afraid we didn't reach deep enough into their hearts where the poison of prejudice festered. I guess we did a good job of helping the participants become politically correct. I only wish I had known about the Institutes for the Healing of Racism at the time.

While spearheading our anti-racism campaign in Nova Scotia, I read a book entitled *To Be One: A Battle against Racism,* written by my long-time friend and associate Nathan Rutstein. I was deeply touched by Nathan's personal candor and integrity. With dignity and courage he disclosed how he had discovered his own infection of racism. His account was personal, respectful, sensitive, and heartfelt. As I finished reading it I felt compelled to phone Nathan to tell him how the book had affected me. I felt he had made an important contribution to the literature on race relations. I found liberating his description of the subtle ways in which racism manifests itself in various guises in the hearts of many Whites. My experience with White people is that denial is most profound among them when it comes to the issue of racism. The precursor to racism is a belief or feeling of superiority toward others of darker skin color. While Nathan understands this, I am puzzled as to why so many White Canadian and United States citizens do not grasp this reality.

On Being on Display and Invisible

Quite a few years ago I read a guest editorial in *Ebony* magazine in which the author, an African-American male, made a comment that attracted my attention. He said, tongue in cheek, that if he could return to this life as a reincarnated being, he would choose to return as a White man. I paused, wondering what were his reasons for such a wish. Why would any African-American man, I asked myself, want to live this life as something other than an African-American man? The editorial writer declared that as a White male he could do almost anything without experiencing recriminations and societal condemnations. He pointed out that if a White man is convicted as a serial killer, Americans and Canadians do not look upon all White men as potential serial killers. However, if the person convicted of being a serial killer is an African-American male, then the tendency is for the general population to become fearful of African-American males. Perhaps this is the reason I experience such a tremendous sense of relief when the news media reports that the person convicted of such heinous crimes is a White man.

In case someone might think that I am exaggerating, simply recall President Bush's war on drugs. He focused on the African-American section of Washington, D.C., giving the impression that drug use and drug dealing was an important aspect of the African-American community. The President's anti-drug initiative also gave the impression that the most dangerous drug dealers are African-American males operating in African-American ghettoes.

When it comes to projecting negative generalizations about African Americans, in particular about African-American males, we find ourselves on display. If there is any hint of drug activity, the news media swarms all over our communities looking for sound bites that reinforce the existing stereotypes. We are put on display when there are social upheavals in or near African-American ghettoes. Remember the riots in Watts, New York City, Detroit, Washington, D.C., and more recently south central Los Angeles. It left us with images of African Americans out of control. No mention was made that the majority of African Americans were not involved in the rioting, that they were opposed to any form of violence, that they were law-abiding citizens. Speaking of lingering images, what about the O.J. Simpson trial? As far as I'm concerned, that trial tried all African-American males, leaving the majority population with the idea that all African-American males are potential wife-beaters and rapists.

As an African American, I feel as if I am on display during everyday occurrences. For example, whenever I walk the streets of the United States and Canada I feel as if I am on display. I can see fear in the eyes of White men and women. I've become sensitive enough to detect the halt in a person's gait when they see me and my sons approaching. White women draw their purses against their body when they see me coming toward them. In order to survive in a hostile society, you learn how to observe the behavior of a potential oppressor, and you learn what kind of face to exhibit so you won't scare the White person. We are continually faced with the challenge of making White folks feel good.

I have had to teach my sons how to do that. I've asked them to be attentive to such matters without being overly stressed. I've had to explain to them why it is necessary to resort to that kind of behavior. To ease potential problems, I have encouraged them to step out of line and look the other way when they see a White woman approaching. This advice is given so they don't end up where the Chicago teenager Emmet Till ended up in the 1950s. While visiting relatives in Mississippi, he was accused of "eyeing" a white woman in a general store. It didn't take long before a group of white men kidnapped the youngster and lynched him.

Because I have had the privilege of obtaining a university education and have attained professionally, I sense that Whites expect me to behave like a White male. Frankly, I reject resorting to that kind of behavior. I want to feel free to express my views with the full force of my being, to take social action on matters of vital import to me, and to fight for justice for all. For the most part, I've been able to do that. Liberal-minded as well as openly prejudiced men and women have told me that I am "too uppity to be Black!" A fair number of them have complained that I express myself with too much passion and conviction. The implication is that I should speak in a monotone, be more reserved, so that I make White people feel more comfortable. I have puzzled over what I should do with such comments and observations. The fact that I like hip-hop music, that I listen to jazz, the blues, soul, American Indian, and African music, that I play this music in my office—has been the subject of much gossip in my workplace. The fact that I communicate, both in writing and orally, in a manner that gives expression to what is in my heart and soul has disturbed some of the people who have worked for me as well as those to whom I report. I find myself not only on display, but in the eyes of Whites, whatever I do is representative of all of the African Americans and African Canadians who exist on our planet. That burden is too much to endure. Out of a need to survive emotionally I continually make efforts to free myself of that burden. I no longer restrain myself when I think I'm being patronized or made to feel that I'm representing every person of African descent in the world. I know that many Whites don't appreciate my candor. I can no longer pretend. To be free is to be yourself. It is important to note that being myself does not mean that I'm prone to assaulting those who are patronizing me or acting superior. Through my racial healing experience I have become more secure as a human being. This allows me to be calm and still be forthright.

It's strange that while I sometimes feel as if I'm on display, there are other times when I am made to feel like a malevolent character in a crime novel. For example, such a feeling and apprehension begin to well up within me when I find myself in a neighborhood that has no African-American residents. I have to ward off the desire to flee. Based on past experience, I know that inevitably I will have to endure the look of the White residents who seem to be saying, "Boy, what are you doing in this area?" Sometimes I feel as though I am suspected of casing or prospecting the area for future illicit activity. These White folks don't see the real me; they see and react to the social projection and stereotype of a criminal. The fact that I am an educated, law-abiding, employed individual who is a husband and father does not seem to enter their mental frame of reference, which is influenced by media projections of negative racial stereotypes. Let's suppose, in the name of fairness, that homes in our predominantly white neighborhood had been robbed. And let's say that the police suspect African-American men as the culprits. It could be reasonably argued that homeowners in the area have a reasonable basis to become apprehensive when they see an unknown African-American man in their neighborhood. On the other hand, if the suspected thieves are White men, those same neighborhood people do not necessarily experience anxiety when an unknown White male shows up. Why is that? I ask myself. Not much effort on my part is required to come up with the answer. I have been conditioned to believe that the White reaction to an African-American man in their neighborhood is the result of a profound, deeply ingrained sense of superiority that manifests itself as racism in all aspects of life in North America. When a member of a group that is considered superior to others deals with a member of the "inferior" minority, they do not have to concern themselves with the personhood of individuals. The individual of color is perceived and responded to as a member of a "collective"—the "inferior" set of folks. This is how slaves in North America were viewed. Thus when American Indians and Africans were enslaved, their demise was of little consequence. The masters and overseers of that time did not have to treat them as equals because the U.S. Constitution viewed them as only three-fifths human. The legacy of this attitude and belief in inherent superiority and inferiority continues to exercise its pernicious and enervating influence in today's society.

There are times when I feel that as an African-American man I am invisible to Whites. These folks don't know me, and I suspect they have no desire to get to know me as a human being. To illustrate the point, I'll share an experience I had during a trip from Colorado to Arizona with some of my friends—four American Indians and one White chap. When we got to our destination, we were not only tired but hungry. We stopped at the first restaurant we saw. By the time I got to the cafe's door, my friends were coming out. "What's up?" I asked. "Oh, when they saw you coming," my White buddy exclaimed, "they said they wouldn't serve us because of you. So we left." It was my first experience at being denied service at a restaurant in America. It would not be my last. To the person who refused to serve us because of me, I, as a human being—the true me—was invisible. He was responding to his own personal and social construct of an African-American person. It didn't matter that I was serving in the U.S. Air Force at the time, or that there was a high probability that I would be going to Vietnam to fight for America.

Discovery

I had heard about the Institutes for the Healing of Racism for approximately six years before Nathan asked me to co-facilitate one with him. Actually, I was surprised that he had asked me to join him in his racial healing venture. At first I was hesitant to accept the offer because I had heard some negative things about the Institutes for the Healing of Racism. Granted, the information came from people who had never experienced the process. Nevertheless, I did not want to get embroiled in a confessional exercise in which people berate themselves and wallow in guilt.

I'm glad that Nathan persisted. I said yes to his suggestion that he spend a weekend with me in my home, where he would explain in detail what the Institutes for the Healing of Racism were all about. His sincerity and the proof of the Institutes' success in achieving their goals swayed me. I later discovered that the rumors that had been circulating about the Institutes were false.

My first experience as a facilitator was shaky. It took place in the fall of 1997 in Detroit, at Starr Commonwealth's center, where thirty-four of its employees were to participate in a two-day racial healing workshop. I had led workshops before, but this was an entirely different kind of workshop. As a co-facilitator, I was expected to participate in the healing process. I was used to being a referee, an objective observer. It was one thing to hear Nathan explain the experience, but it was another thing to experience it.

By immersing myself in the process, I found myself, much to my surprise, revealing feelings I had never shared with others—for example, my search for identity, my need to disabuse myself of feelings of inferiority and to reconstruct myself as a person having an inherent sense of equality, the anger and rage that was deeply buried in my soul. All of this came out despite valiant attempts to prevent it from coming out. At the time I thought I was in complete control, being very cool. I subsequently learned that I was the only one who had thought I was in control. Nathan and others in the group told me that my angst had been written all over my face and was revealed in my body language.

Before long my control defenses broke down. After listening to the heart-wrenching stories of the other participants, I felt as if I were being driven by my soul to release what was pent up in my heart. It poured out.

The only person with whom I had shared my racial struggles up to this point was my wife, Cindy. But in Detroit I revealed stuff that even Cindy was unaware of. A force that came from an unfamiliar place within me moved me to tell my story. I talked about the gang fights, some of which had racial dimensions. I told the group about challenges in school. I described my experience in the Air Force and the discrimination I encountered in Canada. By the time I was finished I was hot. My body temperature had increased, I was sweating, and I felt deep anger. In fact, I was full of rage. Tears began to well up in my eyes, and I began to cry. I had lost it!

I looked over at Nathan beside me and I said, "Man, I lost it. Where are we in the process?" Nathan smiled very lovingly and said, "It's okay." I realized that what I had done was not only okay, it was essential. The "spirit" had, I believe, launched me on the road to healing my internalized racism. I discovered that the process of the Institutes for the Healing of Racism was working for me. Not only did the process assist me to share heartfelt concerns, it also aided me to develop listening skills and a discipline that allowed me to listen and hear others without engaging in mental combat. In fact, I deeply disagreed with some of the contributions made by other members of the group from a historical, social, and, at times, philosophical basis. An urge to confront these individuals swept over me. Because of the Institutes' guidelines for sharing, which do not allow for such exchanges and cross talk or any other confrontational tactic, I kept my mouth shut and made every effort to listen wholeheartedly to the sharing. I was getting to know the real self of the others in the group, and because of that I found myself bonding with them.

One of the things I discovered about the process is that, notwithstanding my angst over something a participant had shared, I found myself exploring my own conscience, asking, What is it, Reggie, about that comment or view that you find so offensive? Why are you allowing it to bug you? Usually the answer to those questions led to the discovery of something linked to my own sense of oppression. This internal examination led me to identify attitudes and emotions I needed to overcome in order to transform.

It took me a number of sessions to understand with my heart something my wife said to me on my fiftieth birthday: "Now that you are fifty, don't you think you can start expressing emotions other than anger? When you are sad, you often express it as anger; when you are hurt you express that as anger; when you are insulted you react angrily." In the Institutes' sessions I have learned to identify more appropriately my emotional responses. What

I found to be even more amazing is that, with the support of the groups engaged in healing racism, I have discovered a newfound courage to admit when I am feeling hurt, sad, or insulted without resorting to anger.

Over the next twelve racial healing sessions I discovered a new sense of confidence in myself. It seemed as if feelings of anger and rage were reduced, as I was able to discover positive outlets to express my feelings, my sense of indignation at the injustice meted out to racial minorities in North America.

The Institutes for the Healing of Racism have another wonderful feature. They make it possible for me to continue my healing through involvement with a group whose members are committed to healing racism within society. I am involved in relationships based on trust with African-American, with White, Hispanic, Asian, and American-Indian men and women.

It is a wonderful feeling to move beyond political correctness, to not have to pretend or walk on eggshells when interacting with Whites. In Institute gatherings I can be myself, my true self. What a relief! I don't have to always talk about "safe" subjects like sports or the weather. I can share my true feelings without having to worry about being condemned or humiliated. To be able to ask questions, even seemingly stupid questions, of one another has been the means of discovery. This could not and would not happen except for the profound level of trust that is developed between the members of an Institute. When trust is established, the foundation for honest communication on real issues is laid. Without trust in and between the members, heartfelt talk and sharing will not occur. With trust everything is possible! This is how I now feel after having been part of twenty-five or more healing racism sessions.

Another important—in fact, essential—part of the Institutes for the Healing of Racism is their ongoing outreach into the community at large.

Once the members of an Institute have advanced along the way to healing their own infection or wound of racism (usually three or four months into the healing process), they are in the position to offer the process to the various institutions within their community such as schools, churches, synagogues, police departments, governmental agencies, and corporations.

I firmly believe that reaching out to serve others is an essential requisite for healing. Service to others allows each participant to step aside from his or her normal range of association, to stretch beyond one's personal barriers to reach others. I believe that by doing this we engage our spiritual selves, in turn developing the higher human values of love, trustworthiness, selflessness, to name a few. In fact it could be said that complete healing might not occur if we do not engage in acts of service to others.

While I'm not given to offering personal testimonies about anything, my direct experience with the Institutes for the Healing of Racism moves me to say that I am grateful Nathan asked me to work with him. My healing is well along the way. My wife and children have noticed a marked difference in me. I am more patient with people and issues related to race relations, whereas, before, I would have been dismissive or explosive. I am more able to express myself without cloaking my comments with rage, an emotion that frightens many people.

In the Institutes for the Healing of Racism experience, each participant learns to listen with his or her heart. Each person begins to cultivate his or her own capacity to sense the heartfelt truth in the comments and expressions made by others. Each participant develops a connection with his or her inner self and learns to share from that depth of being. Is it any wonder, then, that the Institutes for the Healing of Racism have been acclaimed for creating bonds of affection, real communication, and lasting friendships between North Americans of different racial and ethnic backgrounds? This has been and continues to be my experience. It is my hope that all Americans and Canadians will have the bounty of participating in the Institutes' transformative process in which they replace the poisonous effects of racial prejudice with a genuine belief in the oneness of humankind. By working toward healing, each person moves closer to becoming an authentic human being.

An Unanswered Question

While I have found this profound pathway to racial healing and am making some headway, I continue to wonder what must it be like to be a White person in North America. I yearn for the experience of having only to concern myself with the ordinary things of life such as meeting my mortgage or rent payments without having to sweat over whether I would even be granted a mortgage or allowed to rent an apartment because of my skin color.

I would like to experience the freedom of choosing a neighborhood to live in simply because I love the surroundings, the house, nearby parks, and the relative safety of the area. It would please me to no end to secure the services of a realtor without having to worry about whether he was going to show me houses in only the "colored" or "mixed race" sections of town. I have nothing against living in such areas; I've lived in them all of my life. I resent, however, the presumption that is made by others about where they think I ought to live.

I cannot conceive of the peace of mind that White parents experience when they send their children off to school. While I attempt not to show my apprehension, I am concerned that my children will experience school-age racist remarks from other children. I sweat over the possibility that they will be drawn into fights over such remarks. And I am not confident that teachers are aware of their own "infection" with the disease of racism. If they do harbor overt or subconscious negative racial feelings, I worry about the psychological and emotional damage they'll do to African-American, Hispanic, Asian, and American-Indian children they interact with daily. I know what was done to me by well-meaning teachers. I still carry the scars.

To experience shopping in a department store or small retail outlet without the security staff watching my every movement is something I long to behold. Whenever I enter a store operated by Whites, I know I'm not really free. Knowing that I am suspected of being a potential thief because of the color of my skin disturbs me, makes me boil. On one occasion, while browsing in a department store with my children, who were under surveillance as well, I noticed a White man stealing some merchandise. After he left I approached the security people who were following us around and told them that while they were focused on my children and me, they had missed snatching a White man who had robbed them blind.

How does it feel to know that when you apply for a job you are being considered simply on the basis of qualifications, experience, and ability? I have never experienced that luxury. Whenever I apply for a job, one of my first thoughts is, "I hope the prospective employer doesn't require a photograph to be attached to the application." If one is requested, I usually write that job off.

If I were in the position of promoting an African-American employee, I would like to be able to do so without worrying about how it would look to White colleagues. A friend of mine was being considered for a senior provincial government position. His immediate supervisor and the person responsible for making the decision was a member of a racial minority. My friend and his potential colleague were not of the same ethnic group, but both were men of dark complexions. The decision-maker told my friend that he was concerned about how it would look if he and my friend were the two senior people in the department. My buddy retorted that no one seemed to worry if two White men or women head a government department, so why should he? Needless to say, my friend did not get the promotion.

Oh, how I long for the simple pleasure of walking down a city street without being viewed by White passersby as a potential criminal. I would like to walk down the street with my sons and not see fear in the faces of White women, both young and old. I wonder what it is like just to be considered simply a human being? Not a menacing African-American man. I long to find out.

I still do not know what it feels like to do well at something without being told I am a credit to my race or, conversely, without it being suggested that my failure at something constitutes a discredit to my race. Will the time ever come when I can speak up for something I believe in without having to worry that Whites may think I am speaking for all of the people of African descent in North America? What will it take for our society to become comfortable with having the two figurines atop a wedding cake be American Indian or African American?

I wish that while going to college I had had only to worry only about doing my best. Instead I had to worry about whether my poor grade was the result of a racially prejudiced teacher or, if I did well, whether the teacher was on some sort of affirmative action crusade.

Over the course of my life I have applied and competed for many jobs. It would truly be an experience of freedom to be concerned only with having to perform well at the interview and not with worrying about whether the person who is interviewing me is prejudiced toward African Americans. Or to have to stoop to exhibiting the most White-like behavior. I wish I could just be me in a job interview.

I would love to walk down the street, any street, without cringing and growing anxious when I see a police car approaching. I would love not to have to make every White person feel good in order to avoid humiliation.

To be presumed incompetent by other staff members when taking a new position can be devastating. I have experienced that even when assuming the chief executive officer's position. Because of my skin color, the staff assumed that I couldn't do the work of my predecessors, who were all White males. This was manifested in simple ways. For example, staff would correct my written correspondence, claiming my approach was not like that of my predecessors. They tried to educate me about various aspects of the culture of the organization I was heading. It didn't matter to them that I was trying to introduce a new, more dynamic style. They attempted to explain to me why certain things I wanted to do could not be done. Finally, I confronted the staff. In our consultation it became evident to many of the workers that their attitude toward me was sparked by their unconscious sense of racial superiority. Deep down they felt that I was not up to functioning as a chief executive officer of their organization. As a result they felt compelled to come to my aid. It will be a glorious day when my children will not have to put up with such nonsense!

I yearn to live in a world in which I can enjoy what I call "pink perks." I call them "pink" because there is no one who is really "white." Pink perks are the privileges that White folks enjoy unconsciously. They take for granted those simple chores, duties, and practices that people like me find extremely stressful to carry out. People of African descent, as well as American Indians, Hispanics, and Asians carry this extra burden every day of their lives.

In this new millennium these questions still haunt me: What would it feel like to experience life in the United States and Canada as a White person? What would American Indians, Asian Americans, Hispanic Americans, and people of the African diaspora residing in both countries be capable of achieving if that extra burden were lifted from our shoulders and hearts?

—REGINALD NEWKIRK

NATHAN'S STORY

There was a time when I felt that racism was so deeply rooted in the United States that it would take a miracle to uproot it. Any effort on my part to overcome this social malady would be a waste of time and energy. Thinking about the problem always frustrated me as a young adult, and the frustration led to anger and sadness.

The anger would flare up whenever I read about the crimes committed against African Americans, American Indians, Hispanics, and Asian Americans during the formative stages of my country's development. Knowing that the United States' government, from its inception, had consciously and deliberately engaged in an effort to degrade people of color angered me. I was aware that the degradation had often taken the form of legalized mayhem, murder, and seizure of property. The idea was to put America's minorities in places where they would be useful to the ruling Whites but not equal to them.

This knowledge infuriated me, yet I felt powerless to do anything to change the social pattern. After all, I thought, Who am I? Just one man who felt that it was about time something constructive be done to change the racial condition of my country.

I was sure there were others who felt the same way, but I knew we were a fragmented minority. Even if we were to unite, our voice would be too weak to penetrate the mighty sanctums of America's leadership, which is steeped in a tradition of social inequality. Resorting to violence would not help; that would be a suicidal foray and, worse yet, would further divide the nation.

To complicate matters, I realized that, despite all of my country's flaws, there was much that was good about America. People from all over the world were trying to come to our country to partake of its freedoms and opportunities for growth, not only materially and intellectually, but spiritually as well. There is religious freedom in America. While in elementary and high school, I had proudly sworn my allegiance to the United States. I believed that George Washington never told a lie. When my fifth-grade class visited the Statue of Liberty, I sensed a greatness about my country that was unequaled anywhere else in the world. My parents, who had immigrated to the United States from Russia, looked upon their adopted land as a refuge from repeated pogroms—a place where they and their children could "amount to somebody." It had been drilled into me to be proud and protective of my country.

After college, however, I became acquainted with some of America's shortcomings. What I learned then was a far cry from what I had learned in school. At first I didn't want to accept what I read as the truth. I didn't want to believe that the country I loved was fundamentally racist. The Declaration of Independence and the Constitution were documented visions of great promise, but I learned that my government had not lived up to some of its promises. It had not treated a certain block of citizens as Whites' equals, and this was causing terrible suffering and pain to people who only wanted an unrestricted opportunity to develop their human potentialities.

Today there is no doubt in my mind that the greatest American short-coming is racism. Were we to overcome it America would truly become "the land of the free and the home of the brave." Only then would it become a legitimate model of what a nation should be. Only then would America reach its potential greatness. By "greatness" I do not mean "greatness" in the conventional sense, but the greatness that results from a society in which true justice reigns, in which love and unity are the rule rather than the exception.

But my knowledge wasn't going to right the wrongs of the past; it wasn't going to alter the racist collective consciousness of my country; and it wasn't going to remove the poison of racial prejudice from people's hearts.

Why? Because even people with the best of intentions were afflicted by the disease of racism, and that included me. Yes, me! I, who had always wanted to do something meaningful to put an end to the long-standing social injustice in America, I, who was so liberal that when Jackie Robinson had broken into major league baseball I wept, realized that I was afflicted with the disease of racism.

I could distinguish between what was right and wrong. Intellectually, I knew it was wrong to harbor negative racist feelings, but these were feelings over which I knew I had no control. The discovery that, deep down, I harbored these feelings was the source of much shame. Not wanting to believe I was tainted, I tried hard to conceal from everyone, including myself, that I, like so many other White men and women, remained racially tainted.

It angers me to think that I had no choice as to whether I would be infected by the virus of racism. Born and raised in America, I was exposed to a diseased atmosphere that extended from border to border and coast to coast. I, like everyone else I knew, picked up the germ. I can't pinpoint when and how, but I do have some idea of when it became apparent to me that I was afflicted with this social malady that is damaging the heart of the country I love.

Expressway Incident

The incident that brought this awareness took place on a busy expressway. I was in my early twenties, eager to make it to an appointment on time. The driver ahead of me was plodding along at about forty miles per hour. I knew that if I continued at that rate I would be late for my date with a potential client. Heavy traffic made it impossible for me to go around the creeping car ahead of me. Furious, I pressed on the horn. But that had no effect on the driver. Wanting to see who the driver was so I could cuss him out, I arched over the steering wheel and peered through the windshield. The driver was an elderly African-American man. Without hesitation the words "Move, nigger!" flashed through my mind. Anger and hatred toward a person I didn't know welled up in my heart.

I was horrified to realize that I could think and feel that way. After all, I had always been a liberal person, even as a child. I championed the causes of the oppressed and downtrodden. (I wasn't yet aware that such attitudes were based on a subtle sense of superiority, a benevolent form of White burdenism.) It scared me to think that I had no control over these racist thoughts and feelings. I had been caught off guard. Why, I had been so politically correct that the word "nigger" had never passed my lips. In fact, I could honestly say that the ugly word wasn't even in my conscious vocabulary bank. Where did those negative racist thoughts and feelings come from? I wondered in horror. I was so ashamed of myself that I forgot about making the appointment on time. It didn't matter that I was still plodding along at about forty miles an hour. I was faced with a far more important issue than securing a sale. I wanted to find a way to stop the car in front of me so I could apologize to the driver. But that was impossible.

Out of desperation I plunged into denial. An inner voice started to list all of the wonderful things I had done in the human rights field. It didn't take long for me to rationalize the horrible experience I had had. The good I had done to help promote the brotherhood of man certainly outweighed my experience on the road, which convinced myself into believing was an aberration that would never happen again. It was a vow I was certain I could keep.

Racial Encounter in Chicago

I was wrong. There were other emotional racial encounters in which the monster of racism would appear, and I would quickly try to shove it back into my unconscious mind. I actually became quite skillful at repressing these episodes. Maintaining my pro-human rights image was the primary motivation, but my efforts finally failed me. A traumatic experience in Chicago caused all of my liberal defenses to crumble, and the poison of racial prejudice poured out of my heart, encompassing my entire being. At that point I knew that there was no place to hide the fact that I was afflicted with a malady that I didn't choose to have, a malady I had observed and criticized in others. I was beside myself because not knowing how I caught the disease of racism meant that there was no cure for it.

Today I'm grateful for having endured that traumatic experience in Chicago, for it freed me from the stranglehold of denial. I had taken the first step toward healing. Of course, at the time of that experience I wasn't aware that I had taken that first step.

It was the beginning of the summer of 1953, and I was unemployed. Maybe, I thought, I should take up my friend Bill's invitation to come for the summer to Chicago, where jobs were plentiful. If I liked the place I might make the move permanent.

I purchased a one-way train ticket. When I reached my destination I called Bill, thinking I would surprise him. But it was I who ended up being surprised, because Bill revealed that he sensed I would be coming out to Chicago and proceeded to sublet an apartment in the near north side of the city, an area known for its fine restaurants and nightclubs. There was more to the surprise. Bill added that I would have an apartment mate who would share living costs with me. "Great!" I exclaimed and thanked him profusely.

When I knocked on the front door of my apartment-to-be, the door opened and, standing before me was my friend Bill and my prospective apartment mate, Peter, who was African American and very dark. I was shocked, though I tried not to show it, because I didn't want them to know my true feelings. I needed to preserve my liberal image. I smiled and extended a hand of friendship to Peter, who grasped it without hesitation. Evidently Bill had informed him of my reputation as an active advocate of racial equality.

While in the furnished apartment I drank soda with Bill and Peter and engaged in harmless banter, even exchanging jokes, but all the while I was thinking of ways to bow out of the living arrangement without hurting anyone's feelings. I could always pretend that my mother or father had taken seriously ill and that I had to return to New York. Or I could say that a great job opportunity had opened up for me in California or Alaska. I felt that I couldn't live with Peter, even though I knew very little about him. All I knew was that he was taking courses at DePaul University during the day and was driving a bus at night to earn tuition money. I had taken for granted that my apartment mate would be White. While I considered myself a social activist, I had never really socialized with African Americans. I had done favors for some African-American classmates or associates, and I took pride in doing that. But I had no close friends who were African American.

Actually, the thought of living with Peter scared me. I wasn't sure that I would be physically safe living in the same apartment with him. Though desperate, I kept smiling, pretending to be pleased with the living arrangement. We even agreed as to who would take the bedroom of the three-room flat. I said I didn't mind sleeping on the pullout couch in the living room, knowing full well I didn't plan to spend one day in the apartment. Also, by giving up the bedroom, I was able to demonstrate my advocacy of affirmative action.

All of my plotting and scheming proved to be fruitless because I didn't have enough money for a train ticket to New York. I needed to find a job right away, and to do that I needed a place to stay. The only place I knew of was the apartment I had to share with an African-American man.

At the time, I couldn't appreciate the benefits I would derive from sharing the apartment with Peter. My fear, born of ignorance and involuntary racial conditioning, forced me to focus on self-preservation. In the beginning, I couldn't appreciate Peter's thoughtfulness, patience, wonderful cooking ability, and rich sense of humor. He could size up people, too. When it was safe to be open, Peter revealed to me that he had been aware of my true feelings about African Americans on the day he first met me. He said he had not backed out of the living arrangement because he felt that deep down I was a decent guy.

During the first two weeks of living with Peter, I felt like a hypocrite, a traitor to the cause of racial unity, and far from being a decent person. My nights were horrific. I would go to bed around 11:00 P.M., but I wouldn't go to sleep until Peter came home between 2:30 or 3:00 A.M. I would pretend that I was asleep when he entered the apartment. Only when the lights were off in his room would I relax and drift off. The lack of sleep was taking its toll on my job as a butter cutter in a butter factory. I had to be at my work post at 7:00 A.M. It was a half-hour bus ride to get there.

Those nights were horrible because I was afraid of falling asleep, and I wrestled with the shame that resulted. I found myself in terrible conflict. I couldn't sleep for fear that Peter would come home with drunken African-American friends who would beat me up and slit my throat. Though I knew it was wrong to feel this way, these feelings possessed me. At the time, no amount of reasoning and rationalizing could relieve me of these ugly thoughts. Wallowing in self-pity can be awfully painful, especially if you have no control over that state of being.

It took about two weeks before I broke the sleeping pattern. Getting to know Peter helped me to break out of my neurosis. It was the heart-to-heart discussions, eating out and going to the movies, assisting him in cooking Sunday dinner that drew us close together. Getting to know some of his friends, one of whom was White, also helped to cement our friendship. They were all deep-thinking men. Some of our discussions were among the most stimulating I have ever had. I learned a lot, especially from Peter's brother-in-law, who was working on a Ph.D. in sociology at the University of Chicago.

Through our relationship I grew to appreciate Peter's culture. The first time he took me to the neighborhood where he had been brought up I felt uneasy. It was all African American. A month later I was traveling to the South Side of Chicago on my own. Peter's mother was a better cook than her son. But feasting on soul food wasn't the only reason for hopping a subway to the South Side. I started dating Cora, one of Peter's cousins.

My experience with Peter that summer was enriching in many ways. While there were lots of laughs, good meals to share, wonderful conversations, I gained a deep appreciation of what an African American must endure while living in a racist society. So much of what I took for granted was a constant challenge and often a threat to someone like Peter. As a bus driver he had to negotiate the White world almost every day, and every day he was the target of insults, rejection, or—worst of all—complete non-recognition, as if he were some inanimate object, a machine, a slave-robot designed to do the White man's bidding.

While there were no segregation laws in Chicago, Peter learned through advice from older African Americans what he could or couldn't do outside of the South Side. He would never, for example, frequent a barbershop in a White neighborhood unless he was looking for a job shining shoes. And he would never try on a suit or hat in a clothing store outside of his neighborhood. Hailing a taxi cab was an absolutely futile exercise.

Chicago's unwritten segregation laws finally caught up with us near the end of the summer. Tenants in our apartment building complained to the landlord that we were holding multiracial orgies, and they demanded that we be ousted from the flat we were subletting. Of course there was no truth to the charges. We did hold a few parties at which African Americans, American Indians, and Whites gathered, but no liquor was served, no one even smoked, and there was no dancing. There was, however, lots of laughter.

We sensed that some of the tenants were upset with us after a certain incident in mid-August. It involved an elderly woman who lived in the apartment below us. She probably shared what she saw with others in the building.

I believe it was on a Saturday around noon when Peter and I invited his girlfriend, Ernestine, and Cora over for lunch. As we were approaching our place, the downstairs neighbor and her little fox terrier were descending the front stairs. When she spotted us she stopped in her tracks. Though we greeted her warmly, there was no response from her. I guess her feelings were reflected through her dog's snarling and snapping.

The woman followed us up to the second floor and watched us open the door and enter our apartment. A few seconds later we heard her slam her door shut. My guess is that she immediately phoned others to tell them what she had just witnessed.

We were given forty-eight hours to leave the premises. Neither my college friend Bill nor the person he had subleased the apartment from could help us. In those days (the mid 1950s) there were no government agencies to complain to.

Fortunately, the day we moved out was mild, with relatively low humidity and without a cloud in the sky. I didn't think of it at the time, but it was a preview of autumn. Our last chat took place on the building's stoop.

It was early morning, before most people headed for work. My suitcase was beside me. Peter's two satchels, which probably contained everything he owned, were at the foot of the stoop. At first we didn't say anything. We just sat there, thinking.

I don't know who started it, but we began to laugh. Obviously, it wasn't a funny situation, yet we were laughing. To this day I don't know why we were laughing. The only thing I could remember is that it felt good to laugh.

Peter dug into his pocket for his watch.

"What time is it?" I asked.

"About a quarter to seven."

"When do you have to be at work today?"

"Four this afternoon," Peter said, rewinding his watch.

"Have you found a place to live?" I asked.

"Not yet."

"Then where will you go after work?"

"The South Side."

"To your mother's?"

"No . . . But I'll find a place," he said, standing up. "What about you? Are you heading home?"

"In about four hours."

"What do you plan to do when you get there?"

"My mother called the other day to say the *Journal American* in New York wants to interview me for a job as a cub reporter."

"I'm sure you'll get the job."

Peter and I shook hands, and he headed for the subway station.

I never saw him again.

I can't speak for Peter, but the Chicago experience helped me to make some progress in my racial healing struggle. I learned a lot. I gained some idea of what it was like to be an African American in the United States— what privileges came to me simply because I was White. I could now identify some of the invisible barriers that exist between African Americans and Whites. Before going to Chicago I had not been aware of their existence. While I didn't know what it would take to tear down the barriers, I knew that they had to be torn down before racial equality and peace could be realized.

The most meaningful benefit from my relationship with Peter was learning about my real racial condition, and that helped me to gain a better understanding of my true self. I was able to break out of the comfortable embrace of denial. I understood why I had been drawn to such a practice. I couldn't countenance the idea of being affiliated in any way with an evil that I wanted in the worst way to see eradicated. I became a warrior against bigotry and developed my own hate list: the Ku Klux Klan, all "rednecks," Nazis and their sympathizers, isolationists, and social conservatives. All of my energy was directed at defeating the external enemy. None of it was directed at the enemy within me. In retrospect, I think I now know why. Deep down I was afraid of what I would find. Even after that highway experience with the elderly African-American driver, I had fooled myself into thinking that I was free of racial prejudice. Thanks to my Chicago experience, I now know that was a lie.

The Search for a Solution

While I left Chicago liberated from denial, I knew that I was still infected by the virus of racism. I vowed to find ways to heal myself. That was a meandering, often frustrating and painful experience. I tried reading about the problem. That was helpful because I gained a deeper understanding of how racism came into being and what psychological damage it did to the oppressed as well as to the oppressor. I learned how racism had become a powerful element in American culture. Sadly, I discovered that I had been brainwashed about the history of America by good teachers, just as they had been brainwashed by their teachers, and they by their teachers before them.

What I couldn't find in the books was a solution. Reading reinforced my militancy and frustration. I felt like a soldier who was convinced of who his enemy was, anxious to charge ahead, but ignorant of where to go and what to do once he got there.

I sought out people I respected who were progressive-minded and outwardly sympathetic to human-rights causes. All of these White men felt that I was too hard on myself, that the problem was too deep-rooted to change in our lifetime, if ever. They prescribed a course of toleration and advised me to expend my energy in trying to build bridges of respect between cultures. Creating and maintaining social tranquility throughout society, they said, is all that we can accomplish during these dangerous times. To do what I wanted to do, they added, would only lead to disappointment.

I couldn't accept their advice. To follow it, I felt, would be copping out.

I thought that perhaps seeking out the experts in the race relations field would help. I discovered that there was a great variety of experts among the Whites and minorities. Many of them were well intentioned, but there was an assortment of hucksters, both African American and White, who turned the problem of racism into a lucrative business. For a high fee they would guarantee ways to keep a diverse workforce or student body from creating racial tensions and upheavals. I discovered that these glitzy operators have no idea of how to eliminate the core of racism, nor do they have any interest in finding out.

The idealists I sought out identified with various ideological camps devoted to peace and the defense of human rights. The trouble was that they had divergent ways of achieving the same goals. Consequently, they often berated one another in public or behind closed doors. They spent most of their time promoting their concepts and belittling the ideas of their competition. As a result, they made little meaningful headway in ridding the nation of racism. In fact, their behavior and open infighting had a negative effect on those who were less willing to think about the problem of racism in their country. Instead of winning them over to the cause, the idealists alienated most of White America and ended up reinforcing racist views.

It didn't take long for me to understand why. While trying to find a reliable source of healing, I explored some of the different ideological camps, talking with the adherents. There were the White flower-children types who went around preaching peace and love. To get into a loving and peaceful mood they relied on heavy dosages of amphetamines and LSD.

Then there were those who claimed to live on a higher spiritual plain than the average churchgoer. They believed that by continuously exuding unqualified love you could transform a hater into a lover. At first, meeting these people was encouraging. But it didn't take long to realize that most of these White people rarely ventured out of their inner circle. They preferred meditating to moving into the trenches where the human-rights struggle was going on. Most of the love they expressed was toward one another. They had little understanding of the suffering and pain the traditional targets of racism were enduring, and they showed little interest in finding out. What was especially irritating was their impression that they had a special hotline to God. I sensed that their expression of love was more of an act than a genuine expression.

The Marxists didn't need drugs to get their message across. Nor did they possess a monkish mentality. They weren't bashful about promulgating their beliefs and seeking converts. While the different factions had the same aim— complete social equality—their strategies in achieving the aim differed. The Trotskyites called for a bloody revolution. Possessed of total faith in their political philosophy, certain communist ideologues believed that they could persuade the masses to abandon their allegiance to a racist government and embrace Marxism. Other elements tried to infiltrate and sabotage American institutions. In trying to achieve their objectives all of the factions adhered to the end-justifies-the-means principle. They preyed upon the most oppressed and depressed elements of the country, thinking they would flock in droves into communism. All of the factions tried hard to recruit African Americans into the communist camps. Special emphasis was given to attracting highly educated African Americans in the hope that they would lead all other African Americans in a sustained revolt against the government. Most African Americans rejected this call from the extreme left.

Then there were the White liberals who engineered the multicultural movement. Their idea was to get people to respect and appreciate ethnic, religious, and racial differences. A great deal of money and effort were expended to organize situations in schools, churches, synagogues, and fraternal societies that would bring together different ethnic groups, races, and religions, featuring their favorite foods, costumes, dances, and songs. By organizing regular festivals of diversity, they believed, different kinds of people would develop friendships, thus putting an end to racism and anti-Semitism.

I found such efforts superficial and essentially counterproductive. An exchange of cultural artifacts isn't going to purge racism and suspicion from people's hearts. As a result of the emphasis on cultural pride, many ethnic groups developed toward others a sense of superiority that often evolved into subtle prejudice. Much effort was required to conceal one's true feelings toward members of other ethnic, religious, or racial groups. Political correctness was fostered and practiced with great enthusiasm. I was discouraged to find that many devoted multiculturalists were opposed to the principle of the oneness of humankind. Despite modern science's insistence that all human beings are biologically related to one another, that there is only one human race, the multiculturalists resist embracing this reality as if it were a plague. Since prejudice is an emotional attachment to ignorance, these people, I concluded, were prisoners of prejudice, and they didn't know it. In time I discovered that some elements among these people resisted oneness for fear that it would lead to unity. Unity, they felt, could easily lead to the diminishing of their culture and advantage in society. In reality, these people were cultural separatists, operating in public as promoters of respect for all cultures. Fortunately, most people of color could see right through the masquerade.

Seeking enlightenment from African-American idealists was equally frustrating. I found many factions among them. Like their White counterparts, their differences were ideological. Many, especially those who were members of the middle class, aligned themselves with the mainstream NAACP and the Urban League, two well-established civil-rights organizations that seek social and economic equality through legal and political means. Little effort was made to change people's racial conditioning. I got the impression that the leadership wasn't interested in creating transformational programs because of their belief that changing hearts was impossible. Their major thrust was winning equal opportunity for America's minorities.

I sensed that winning equal opportunities wasn't going to be enough. The civil-rights laws of the 1960s offered a case in point. Though the laws were needed, they didn't remove the hatred, anger, fear, and suspicion that racism generates in human hearts. As a consequence, the powerful have found ways to circumvent the laws. Public education provides an example. In the 1960s and 70s Whites fled the inner cities for the suburbs, leaving the schools populated with students of color and a few Whites who were too poor to move elsewhere. In smaller towns and rural areas private academies were established, usually by churches, as a means of avoiding racial integration in schools.

Conflicts in the African-American Community

Within the African-American community there is still conflict between the way W. E. B. DuBois and Booker T. Washington approached the challenge of winning true equality for African Americans. DuBois demanded immediate racial equality and justice through the force of law. Washington, a gradualist, suggested that African Americans prove their ability to function effectively in a democracy by mastering the trades. Though the debate started in the early twentieth century, and although DuBois and Washington have been dead for many years, both social activists have followers today who continue the heated debate.

Adherents of the Black Power movement, for the most part, have given up trying to integrate into White America. But different factions have different reasons for not wanting to assimilate into America's mainstream. One faction feels that social integration would mean having to reject one's culture and become a White person with an African face. At the same time, if the White community were to agree to scrap existing social mores and work with African Americans and other minorities on a truly equal basis to create a new set of mores founded on true equality, then and only then would they favor integration. But they don't hold out much hope that Whites will take such a drastic step. Instead, these idealists are trying to find ways to foster economic, educational, and health development in African-American communities. Though they won't admit it, they are working to set up a truly separate but equal society.

Then there are the adherents of Black Power who have no interest in associating or working with Whites, because they feel that Whites are essentially evil, that they are incapable of freeing themselves of their racial prejudice. Currents of vengeance run through this group, leading to a tendency toward violence among some of these people. Unlike most African Americans, they don't hide their anger toward Whites. In fact, some of them derive pleasure from seeing Whites suffer.

There are also the Pan-Africanists, who advocate returning to an "African way of life." This means scrapping one's given name for an African name, wearing African-style clothing, attending Afrocentric schools, becoming acquainted with African cultures, and abandoning Christianity for religions that are native to the countries from which their ancestors came. Most Pan-Africanists refuse to socialize with Whites.

Religion in the African-American community is, for the most part, a reactionary force. While there are many competing sects, they are united in preventing the amalgamation of African-American and White churches. From time to time an African-American choir and a White choir will sing together in an annual ecumenical event, or an African-American minister will deliver a sermon in a White church and vice versa. But that is sheer tokenism. Few African-American ministers have any real desire to integrate. Nor are the majority of White pastors inclined to share the pulpit with an African-American clergyman on a regular basis. To do so would mean for both a loss of financial security, loss of one's power base in the community, and the loss of a reliable platform for public recognition and adulation.

Because of Islam's growing appeal among African Americans, especially young male adults, African-American Christian ministers view the Muslims as a threat to their security. While they will actively resist any Muslim encroachment in their religious domain, they listen with rapt attention to what the head of the Nation of Islam, Minister Farrakhan, has to say, often cheering the dynamic Muslim leader on for saying publicly what they believe privately. While many African-Americans remain loyal to Christianity, deep down they have greater respect for Minister Farrakhan than for their own pastors.

There is also still prejudice among African Americans. Because of the prevalence of internalized racism, there has long been a pecking order in the African-American community based on the shade of one's skin color. Lighter-skinned African Americans look down on darker-skinned African

Americans and avoid associating with them. Acceptance into African-American college fraternities and sororities have been based on a candidate's shade of skin color. Obviously, this has caused considerable resentment among darker-skinned individuals. For some darker people, such rejection has seriously eroded their self-esteem. At the same time, some darker African Americans who have embraced the "Black is Beautiful" concept openly look down on the lighter-skinned Blacks as not being African enough. They particularly avoid meaningful relationships with biracial men and women, treating them as traitors to the "cause."

Dr. Martin Luther King, Jr.

I have encountered only one African-American man whom I got to know through my work as a journalist who was able to transcend the foibles, the fears, the suspicion and distrust, the internalized racism that plague so many African Americans today. Though he was aware of the struggle required to overcome racism in his country, he was hopeful that one day all Americans would view themselves as members of the same family.

I interviewed Dr. Martin Luther King, Jr., several times. I was impressed with him each time we met. To me, his magnetism didn't come from what he said, though his words were a powerful source of attraction. He could have been sitting in silence and I still would have been drawn to him. Each time we met I learned something new about the man. He was always in control, even when reporters fired sticky questions at him. His response was never harsh, never a put-down; he never resorted to sarcasm. His manner did not change in private; he was consistently sincere. Dr. King exuded a strength that had to come from deep faith, a faith fashioned from a lifetime of reflection and prayer. He didn't have to say he believed in God; being with him you just knew he did.

There was no question in my mind that he knew what he had to do and that he had thought deeply about how he was going to do it. While he had his sight fixed on certain objectives, he would take the time to respond to others' concerns. I experienced his compassion while covering one of his trips to New York City.

After his speech one evening, I and about twenty other reporters rushed to the stage to ask Dr. King questions. With microphones thrust in his face, he calmly responded to the journalists' queries about the civil rights movement. Though I was there to ask the same kinds of questions, I wanted to bring up an issue only indirectly connected to the American civil rights campaign. I wanted to tell him about the persecution of the Moroccan Bahá'ís.

The practical side of me hesitated. How would I explain such an unorthodox action to my editor? But I saw in Dr. King a quality that I admired but hadn't personally developed: He seemed to be someone you could bare your soul to. And that's what I did, amidst a corps of hardnosed reporters who were jockeying for position to ask the appropriate questions.

They must have thought I was crazy when I asked Dr. King if he had heard about the plight of the Bahá'ís in Morocco. His reaction was exactly what I thought it would be. He moved closer to me, his eyes reflecting deep concern. I don't know how long we stood there talking, oblivious of the press corps, the autograph-seekers and other admirers, African-American and White. It was as if I were no longer on assignment and we were engaged in a private conversation. He wanted to know the scope of the persecution and what had precipitated it. He asked what form the persecution had taken and whether anyone had been harmed. When I told him that several Bahá'ís had been sentenced to death for practicing their Faith, he shook his head as if to say, "When will man's inhumanity to man stop?"

An aide came by, pointing to his watch, but Dr. King didn't turn away from me. He continued to listen and then told me he knew some Bahá'ís and that he was impressed with the teachings of the Faith. Before leaving he suggested that the Bahá'ís' leadership take the problem to the United Nations and then asked what he could do to help relieve the pressure on the Moroccan Bahá'ís.

Through that brief encounter with Dr. King, I gained an appreciation of what a human being is capable of attaining spiritually. He was not only universal in his thinking, he was universal in his being. While we were together his attitude freed me from my prejudices. I was lifted into a realm where love dominates, and because of that I was neither fearful nor suspicious nor selfish. I was free.

Unfortunately, that precious feeling didn't last long. And while Dr. King's short time on Earth helped many of us to appreciate the gravity of racism's stultifying effect on America, not much was accomplished toward its eradication. The social condition in America was so fragmented that it was impossible to find even a subtle sign to a solution for the problem of racism. All of the so-called civil rights activity resulted in superficial advancements. While it helped to integrate public places, it failed to purge from human hearts the feelings of superiority and inferiority, fear, suspicion, and hatred that prevented people from genuinely believing in the oneness of humankind.

The Search Continues

I became convinced that without this kind of transformation all of the money and energy spent trying to break down racial barriers won't change the racial conditioning of Americans. Mastering political correctness won't do it. Exchanging cultural artifacts once a year won't do it. Annual race unity picnics won't do it. Nor will wearing T-shirts with anti-racist slogans. What's under the T-shirt—the heart—needs to be healed.

I also became convinced that our country's leaders in education, business, and technology didn't have a clue as to how to put an end to racism. Whatever they did to try to curb the spread of the social malady did not spring from a genuine desire to relieve the suffering and pain that racism inflicts upon America's minorities. Whatever action they took usually came after a serious racial upheaval. Their aim was to make sure another uprising didn't take place and ensure that social tranquility reigned. They became proficient Band-Aid administrators.

These leaders lack a genuine desire to do something truly meaningful about the problem because they haven't dealt with their own racism. Many of them are in deep denial. Because they haven't given the problem the thought it deserves and haven't looked into their own hearts, they are unaware of the true nature of racism. Consequently, the anti-racism or diversity programs they create or support end up being counterproductive. Such programs fail to deal with the core of the problem, leaving African Americans, Hispanics, American Indians, and Asian Americans frustrated and more convinced than ever that there is no solution to the problem. As a result, these minorities become increasingly skeptical toward White-generated race relations efforts. They become convinced that Whites cannot be trusted because they'll never understand what the problem really is and how they contribute to keeping it alive.

Without the wholehearted support of America's minorities it is impossible to heal the disease of racism. Why? Because African Americans, American Indians, Hispanics, and Asian Americans are affected by the disease as well. They are not affected in the same way that Whites are, but they are affected nonetheless. While Whites need to overcome their conscious or subconscious inherent sense of superiority toward their darker-skinned fellow citizens, the minorities need to overcome their internalized racism, their post traumatic stress disorder, their suspicion and paranoia.

Multiculturalism as it is practiced today is counterproductive not only for minorities but for Whites as well. It distracts them from bringing themselves to account, from becoming acquainted with the nature of their racial conditioning. As a result, most of their time is spent promoting tolerance of differences instead of healing their racism and internalizing the reality of the oneness of humankind.

In my search for a healing cure to racism, I became convinced that, since we are all affected by racism in America, we need to work together in healing ourselves. Overcoming racism is everyone's responsibility. But to accomplish that end there has to be a committed core of men and women who understand the nature of the problem and are willing to engage in a timeless healing process. If genuine transformation takes place, those outside the healing circle will take notice and will want to get involved.

I finally found what I was looking for. But that awareness only came after a series of events. At the time I was going through them, I had no idea they would lead to a program that would accelerate my own healing and draw together as brothers and sisters people who had once distrusted, even hated, each other. Maybe the formation of the Institutes for the Healing of Racism was a miracle.

Marc's Story

It started for me with a racial incident at nearby Northampton High School in Northampton, Massachusetts. Several human rights advocates and I banded together to determine what had caused the student upheaval in an effort to create a healthier social climate at the school. The first thing we did was to invite the African-American and Hispanic students and their parents to meet with us at a neutral place. We wanted to find out what it was like for them to live in a predominantly White town and attend school there.

Marc, an African-American lad, was the first to share his feelings. He had left his native Cleveland, Ohio, because his mother had won a scholarship to attend Smith College, which is located in Northampton. Marc said that in the beginning he had been happy about the move because he had heard about Northampton High School's outstanding academic reputation. That was very important to Marc because he loved learning. In Cleveland he had been a straight-A student who loved mathematics and science. He had dreamed of becoming an electrical engineer, an inventor. Back in Ohio he had won a number of awards for inventing a series of electrical gadgets.

But it didn't take long for his high expectations to plummet.

Because of his sterling academic record at his previous high school, the administrators at Northampton High School had no choice but to place Marc in the advanced track. They did this against their better judgment. They were accustomed to placing Hispanic and African-American students in a lower track—one that wasn't dedicated to preparing students for college. Some of Marc's teachers thought that he would feel a lot more comfortable being in school with his "own kind." There was another reason Marc's teachers felt he didn't belong in the advanced track: They were certain that the As he made at the predominantly African-American high school in Cleveland were equivalent to Cs at Northampton High School.

Marc wondered why the teachers rarely called on him in class. He usually knew the answers to the questions they would pose. I later discovered why they often ignored his raised hand. While they liked Marc—for he wasn't rowdy, didn't speak "ghettoized" English, and was well mannered—

they didn't call on him because they didn't want to embarrass the youngster before his peers. They assumed that he didn't know the answers because they weren't accustomed to having an African-American student doing honors work. Because of the school's tracking system, they had been conditioned to believe that students of color were unable to cope with advanced courses. Reinforcing that assumption was the fact that Marc had attended in Ohio a school that they believed to be academically inferior to the one in which they taught.

After three weeks at the new high school, a strange feeling began to sweep over Marc every time he entered a classroom. Even when he sat down at his desk, the desire to flee would possess him. Consequently, he began to gaze at the clock, waiting for the period to end. When he told his mother about the urge to leave class and explained that it was difficult to concentrate there, she countered by telling him that he had to make the best of it, reminding him that with a good education, "you'll achieve your career goals. You'll become an electrical engineer."

While Marc obeyed his mother, the strange feeling didn't disappear. Neither Marc nor his mother were aware of what was happening to him. Marc's situation worsened. About a month after the onset of that strange feeling, something terrible happened to him. He became unable to think or reason in class. This had never happened before. At the time, Marc was too bewildered and embarrassed to tell anyone. Maybe it's just a temporary dysfunction, he thought, and it will go away. But it didn't go away. In fact it followed him home. Every time he opened a textbook to do his homework, he would draw a blank. He wondered if he were losing his mind.

Marc began to cry when he told me that, because he had lost his ability to think effectively, he had been placed in the lower track. The youngster was crying because he felt that his dream of becoming an electrical engineer had been dashed. As I watched Marc crying, an insight came to me that later proved accurate: Marc had been psychologically crippled by well-intentioned teachers in a school he was confident would properly prepare him to achieve his career goals. His teachers didn't share Marc's remorse. They were certain that they had rescued him from an academic place where he didn't belong. In time, they believed, he would feel far more comfortable with his "own kind."

That evening I had difficulty sleeping. The thought that what had happened to Marc was happening to other African-American, Hispanic, American Indian, and Asian-American students across the country plagued me. It was happening every day, and no meaningful steps were being taken to stop the psychological damage. This, I concluded, was a form of genocide.

About three months after the experience with Marc, I discovered why he had lost his ability to think and what had set off that feeling to flee the classroom. While in Hawaii I came across the work being done by human developmentalist Kenneth Yamamoto, who was trying to find out why so many Polynesian youth were dropping out of school. He said that when a student who feels devalued and emotionally upset steps into a classroom, it turns into a factory for failure, and he's seized by an urge to flee. Now that isn't a bad impulse, because it is nature's way of protecting the child from being destroyed intellectually and emotionally. When a student has such an experience repeatedly over an extended period of time, the brain's cerebral cortex, which processes thought and speech, shuts down and the student can't think or reason. When that happens, the part of the brain that controls our emotions sets off one of two survival impulses—fight or flee.

The student who wants to flee either falls asleep in class or becomes emotionally disengaged, often displaying bizarre behavior, which usually leads to suspension or expulsion from school. It is the student's unconscious way of protecting himself from emotional and intellectual destruction.

The student who decides to fight is extremely angry, edging toward violence. Not knowing what is happening to him, his inner voice cries out, "I hate this school, this class, this teacher." He doesn't want to believe he's a dummy. In fact, he knows he's not, but there's no way to convince the teacher that he's a smart kid. Sensing that he has no control over his destiny, he becomes desperate, a ripe candidate for trouble. The teacher, however, responds to the outward expression of the angry, fearful, desperate soul, and, out of self-defense, brands him as a behavioral problem and places him in a special track for the emotionally upset. While he is in that track, the school psychologist gives him mind-numbing drugs, which are designed to restrain him from harming himself or others. In class he goes through the motions of being educated. In order to keep him busy and out of trouble, he is engaged in mindless classroom exercises such as copying textbook prose into a notebook. His meaningless A's and B's on his report card are meant to keep the students' parents from descending on the teachers and principals to demand a better education for their children. If these students don't drop out of school, they graduate with worthless diplomas, unfit to function effectively in what they feel deep down is a hostile democratic society.

After graduation they find themselves facing a crossroads, having to choose between two tracks. If they choose track A, they bow to the educators' evaluation of themselves and say, "Yes, yes, I am a dummy," and spend the rest of their lives looking for ways to dull the pain. Our cities and towns are crowded with men and women who have been psychologically damaged in this way by school systems made up of well-intentioned teachers and principals, people who want to do the right thing, who want to help their students grow intellectually. But, frankly, they do not know how to end the psychological murder and crippling of African-American, Hispanic, American-Indian, and Asian-American students.

The student who chooses track B resists accepting the educators' evaluation of himself. He resists with the seeds of doubt that have been planted in him. During weak moments the thought that the teachers might be right about him flashes through his mind. But he usually gathers his strength and snaps back, continuing to resist. In time, his resistance is not only directed at his teachers' view of him, but at the establishment in general. He resists and resists until he gets in trouble with the law. It is not surprising that more than one-third of all African-American males between the ages of twenty and twenty-nine are either in jail, on parole, or on probation.

A Solution Emerges

My experience with Marc and my sudden awareness of the role formal education was playing in damaging students of color inspired me to explore ways to bring an end to racism. Finding a reliable means of healing my own racism was an added incentive.

I decided to write the book *To Be One: The Battle against Racism,* intending for it to function as a mirror to a White person's soul. My hope was that readers would become acquainted with their own true racial conditioning and summon the courage to liberate themselves from denial's embrace. To accomplish that goal I described how I discovered my infection of racism. Without holding back I revealed in detail my internal struggle to face up to the truth and explained what I had done to try to find ways to heal myself of a virus I had denied having as long as I could remember.

I had some success in reaching my goal, but what impressed me most was a letter I received from a close friend, Dr. Sam McClellan. Sam was a psychiatrist who had taught for years at Harvard's School of Public Health. He was a person of sterling integrity, wholehearted honesty, and pure humility, and he was a genuine lover of humankind. To me he was a model I wanted to emulate. When he and his family had moved to Kentucky, my contact with him had become less frequent, but my book drew us closer.

In his letter Sam revealed that the book had affected him profoundly. He said that, while he was in Cambridge, he had thought he was free of racial prejudice. After reading the book, however, he realized he had fooled himself, that he was indeed infected by racism. Sam admitted that he didn't know how to get rid of it.

Moved by Sam's sincerity and honesty, I called him. After a long, indepth discussion about racism in America, he asked, "What can we do to solve this problem?"

"Let me think about it," I replied.

As soon as I hung up the phone, I berated myself for being so arrogant. Here I was, talking to a psychiatrist and giving the impression that in time I was going to come up with a solution—I, who had never taken a psychology course, never read a psychology text. At that moment I didn't have the foggiest idea of what to do to end the four-century-old plague that was sapping my country's vitality.

I knew for sure that what was already being done in hopes of curing the infection wasn't making any meaningful headway. In fact, a lot of what was being done was counterproductive. (We'll elaborate on this point later.) Taking stock of my feelings about racism, I knew that finding a cure would require the development of something other than what was already being done. I sensed that racism was a sickness—certainly not a bacterial or viral infection, nor an organic defect, but a psychological, emotional, and spiritual problem. Intuitively, I felt that maybe we could deal with racism the way Alcoholics Anonymous deals with alcoholics. The idea felt right.

But some of the mental health professionals I knew in my town didn't think the idea could succeed. In fact, a few of them felt it was a lame-brained idea. Though discouraged, I prayed for help.

About a week after my discouraging survey, I received a phone call from Hitaji Azziz, a woman from Houston, Texas. She was a recovering alcoholic and therapist who had a popular radio talk show. She called me to say that she had been reading excerpts from my book on the air. Because of the positive impact the readings were having on her audience, she felt a group should be organized to help those sincere people who wanted to overcome their racism. When she suggested calling the group "Racism Anonymous," I replied, "You are an answer to my prayers."

A month later I met her and eight others who were committed to developing an ongoing racial healing mechanism. They were a diverse group, mostly women: a Japanese American, two Hispanics, four African Americans, a Persian American, and four European Americans. At that meeting the group decided to call itself the Institute for the Healing of Racism. I liked the name because it included the word "healing." I felt the word indicated the true nature of the problem—an illness—and that the illness could be cured.

The first Institute was established in Houston, Texas, and is still going strong. Since 1989 scores of other Institutes have been formed in continental United States, Canada, Alaska, Hawaii, Great Britain, and Australia. I have had the bounty of witnessing hundreds of participants from all walks of life experience healing and transformation. People who once distrusted each other, even hated one another, have learned to love one another and embrace, often in tears, as brothers and sisters. Seeing that kind of transformation occur time after time has made me optimistic about the possibility of overcoming racism and replacing it with a genuine belief in the oneness of humankind.

My Institute co-facilitator, Reginald Newkirk, has also shared in that bounty. For more than two years we have worked together in Michigan, training more than one thousand people who sincerely want to heal their racism, taking them to the threshold of hope and helping them find a clear view of the path to healing. We have seen Institutes raised up and flourish, and through their efforts new Institutes have been born. We have witnessed the development of a grassroots movement that is now beginning to draw attention from America's leaders, who are desperately seeking help to solve a problem that doesn't seem to go away despite all efforts to get rid of it.

—NATHAN RUTSTEIN

Part 2

GOALS AND AIMS

Desire, enthusiasm, and commitment aren't enough to wage an effective war against an evil such as racism. Proper perspective and focus are required. To achieve that end, those committed to the campaign must have a clear understanding of its goals. They must also have a clear idea of what it takes to achieve those goals and a deep desire to do the job. Otherwise the war will be lost, leaving a battlefield strewn with wounded anti-racism warriors. Healing the wounds of disillusionment, skepticism, and hopelessness is extremely difficult.

Over the years the goals of the Institutes for the Healing of Racism have changed. These changes spring from our experience—often from the mistakes we have made—which has given us new insights about the Institutes' potentialities and their ability to heal and transform.

After years of experimentation, it appears that we now know what the Institutes are capable of doing and what they need to accomplish. There are two goals, which are intertwined:

1. For participants in the Institutes for the Healing of Racism to become healers of racism in the their own communities. To become

an effective healer, you must be involved in the process of healing yourself.

2. For participants in the Institutes for the Healing of Racism to become forces of unity within their communities. You cannot achieve this goal if you are not wholeheartedly involved in trying to achieve the first.

There are five steps to achieving the two goals:

1. To gain an understanding and internalize the realities underlying the principle of the oneness of humankind.

2. To gain an accurate understanding of how racism came into being in our country.

3. To gain an understanding of the pathology of racism and how it affects all of us.

4. To establish on ongoing mechanism for healing whereby participants come together on an equal basis, committed to helping one another heal our infection and wounds of racism in a safe, non-confrontational environment.

5. To engage in social action. When an Institute becomes well grounded, there is a natural urge among its members to set up other Institutes within public and private institutions in the community at large. We view the establishment and operation of Institutes for the Healing of Racism as social action because they are dedicated to eliminating barriers to positive racial individual and societal transformation. Without identifying, focusing on, and working to overcome the core problem of racism, only superficial progress will be made in the war against racism.

While the Institutes are engaged in healing the disease of racism, they are careful not to promote any particular political or economic philosophy or religious creed. The primary focus is on fostering individual and community racial healing and unity.

THE INSTITUTE PROCESS

Each Institute for the Healing of Racism is not a place but instead an ongoing program—in other words, a process. It is held in libraries, college classrooms, churches, city halls, schools, even private homes. Outwardly it may appear as another dialoguing experience that leads to a lot of talk and no meaningful action. True, its purpose isn't to organize protests or human rights marches, nor to lobby for civil rights legislation. Not that doing those things is wrong. There are times when such actions are needed. However, an Institute pinpoints the core of the problem and heals what many people of good will try to hide from the public. In the end, it frees individuals to become lovers of whomever they encounter.

The primary purpose of the Institutes for the Healing of Racism is to engage participants in a process of personal transformation that enables them to purge from their hearts the negative effects of racism, replacing these negative effects with a genuine belief in the oneness of humankind. This usually leads to more love and unity in one's community.

We believe that unless this process of personal transformation occurs, no meaningful strides can be made to overcome racism. While it was good to end racial segregation in public places, very little has been done to overcome the feelings of superiority, inferiority, suspicion, hatred, fear, anxiety, resentment, and frustration of African Americans, Hispanics, Asians, American Indians, and Whites who now line up to use the desegregated water fountain. Because these issues have not been addressed, Americans remain spiritually fragmented, devoting a great deal of energy to avoiding ugly racial encounters and establishing a false atmosphere of tranquility in which various ethnic, religious, and racial groups merely tolerate one another. The point is that such action only addresses the symptoms of the disease and not the disease itself. It also allows those with the greatest political and economic power to devise means of circumventing civil rights laws. Substantial progress will be made when people who resort to such actions no longer feel a need to do so—when all of the energy spent concealing one's true racial conditioning is channeled into quickening the healing process.

An extremely important action usually results for those involved in the Institutes' transformational experience. Often it occurs midway through the training cycle. African-American, Hispanic, American-Indian, Asian, and White participants begin to do things together between sessions. This coming together is perfectly natural, for the participants have gotten to really know each other in intimate ways. By sharing their internal pain and fear in a safe and compassionate atmosphere, their hearts have become connected, free from the burdens that caused the pain and fear of past interracial encounters. As a result, participants long to be with each other. They may go to a movie together, invite each other over to one another's homes for dinner. Their children become friends. There's little or no talk of race. True friendships are forged. But, more than that, through their transformation they demonstrate that it is possible for people who were once distrustful of one another because of skin-color to learn to love each another.

This kind of action doesn't attract national television coverage, nor is it featured in major national newspapers or magazines. Yet in the long run it is more meaningful than rioting, or angrily demonstrating, or even securing the passage of needed civil rights laws. We have had the demonstrations, the parades, the multicultural festivals, the race unity picnics, and we have seen the passage of good laws, but these have done little to change people's racial conditioning. While many Whites believe much has been accomplished toward establishing racial equality in America, most of those who are the traditional targets of racism disagree. Racism is the same, they feel; all that has really changed is the way it is manifested. It is far less overt, but just as painful.

The grassroots movement called the Institutes for the Healing of Racism is helping—peacefully and without the use of high-powered technology— to dismantle a national cultural set of mores based on racial inequality and replace it with a new set of mores based on social justice.

To participants in the Institute process, transformation is the watchword. However, changing one's attitudes and behavior isn't easy. Though we don't openly admit that ours is a racist society, we can't help but sense that it is. To make the best of a condition they cannot control, out of self defense they create a racial mindset that helps them survive in a potentially explosive situation. The White mindset is based on principles arising from a set of survival instincts activated by fear. But this fear does not stem from a sense of inferiority. It is the kind of fear that an unarmed person experiences in a strange forest inhabited by unfamiliar people and animals.

Some of the principles that make up the White person's racial survival mindset, which is essentially a facade, include the following: Avoid talking about race, especially with people of different races. When race does come up in a conversation, try to change the topic. Sharing a politically correct joke usually helps. If it fails to change the topic, it might lessen the tension.

If that is impossible, try to be as complimentary as possible about the race of the person you are talking to. To become proficient in complimenting a member of a different race, become knowledgeable about the scientific, educational, industrial, musical, and athletic achievements of African Americans, American Indians, Asians, and Hispanics. Share that knowledge at appropriate times during interracial activities. Avoid being in places where the majority of people are of a different race. Attend those interracial events at which Whites are a distinct majority. To ensure personal safety and a tolerable degree of social acceptance, give regularly to charities that cater to people of color, and make sure that as many people of color as possible are aware of your donations. Participate in various multicultural events, such as festivals and workshops. Write pro-diversity letters to the editor of the local newspaper. Take advantage of every opportunity to give the impression that you are free of racial prejudice and a real friend of minorities.

Like the White racial mindset, the African-American mindset is fashioned by the need to survive. But the fear that fuels the need is different. It is based on a mountain of doubts and suspicions. The doubts and suspicions can be justified by citing the way African Americans have been treated by Whites for nearly four hundred years and the way African Americans have been forced to behave in integrated settings, particularly at work. Much effort is expended to cover up feelings of alienation that stem from feeling like an outsider in a place where he is officially a member. Deep down, he believes he'll always feel that way, as will his children and their children. To fight for the right to feel that he belongs would take too much out of him. Most likely he has tried in the past and found it emotionally draining. Besides, he rationalizes, his chances of gaining that right are nil. The only thing he'll gain from such an effort is a sense of bitterness and resentment and anger that would turn him into a walking time bomb that could be set off anytime. So most of the time that he spends in the presence of Whites is spent working to make them feel good. This service is not an act of altruism but rather an act of self preservation. Much of his behavior is based on a lie, and in the beginning of this charade he knows it. But after engaging in it year after year, this kind of behavior becomes a way of life, and he's no longer aware of living a lie. His desire to punch out the White guy he is praising has faded away.

The pretense that goes into maintaining both the White and African-American racial mindsets takes its toll psychologically on those who are forced to maintain them. It can easily become a mental health problem, for isn't mental health measured by one's proximity to reality? Repressing your true feelings and creating a set of artificial feelings that you force yourself to believe is real is a way of distancing yourself from reality.

Participants in the Institutes for the Healing of Racism are exposed to a process that helps them dismantle their racial mindset and replace it with a reality-based understanding. In the process, they come to understand the composition of what they are getting rid of as well as why and how it developed. They realize that the mindset was based on rationalizations, myths, fears, conscious and unconscious biases, and pretense.

The sense of liberation that African Americans and Whites experience when they shed their racial mindsets can be experienced by people from a broad spectrum of social philosophies, including unabashed White bigots and Black militant separatists. But those who stand to gain the most are the people in deep denial who try to hide their true racial feelings behind the shield of political correctness, for they must first overcome the delusion that they are not infected by racism and then deal with their infection. White bigots and Black militants have only to deal with their infection.

Most people do not experience instantaneous transformation. To expect that to happen is to expect a miracle. Much effort is required. After all, racism has been around for a very long time. Getting rid of it is, in some respects, like removing a ship's barnacles. Hard work is required. Painting over it (political correctness) won't do it. When the barnacles are removed, the vessel moves smoothly through the water. In the beginning of the healing process, some pain is experienced, much like the mountain climber experiences when ascending a mighty mountain. When the summit is reached, the climber gains a deep appreciation of what it took to gain the sense of freedom and joy he or she now possesses.

Conquering a problem such as racism draws you closer to discovering and developing your true self, a necessary step to functioning as a complete human being. How is this so? Harboring racial prejudice, or any other prejudice, prevents the soul from manifesting its full potential. It doesn't matter how often you attend religious services or contribute to charity. You find yourself operating more on animal power than soul power. If you are not aware of the relationship between the soul and the body, you are not aware of the primary operating force in your life.

Perhaps a metaphor will clarify how racial prejudice and its effects prevent people from functioning the way humans are meant to function. Our Creator, the source of all knowledge and love, can be likened to the sun, while the human soul can be likened to a mirror facing the sun, or God. Potentially, a perfectly clean mirror reflects more of the sun's light than a filthy mirror does. The filth of racial prejudice on a human soul screens out much of the light of God's knowledge and love that's constantly streaming forth. This leaves the human being vulnerable to darker, more animalistic instincts such as avarice, fear, ignorance, and self-centeredness instead of developing in him the higher spiritual qualities such as selflessness, love, compassion, courage and trustworthiness that radiate from the Creator.

Participants committed to the healing process in time not only heal their racism but usually gain insights about the nature of humankind, discover and begin to develop their true selves, and gain a deeper understanding of the purpose of life.

DISTINGUISHING FEATURES

The Institutes for the Healing of Racism are not satisfied with merely helping people of different skin colors to tolerate one another. They are primarily concerned with helping them learn to love one another truly and honestly. To accomplish that goal, the Institutes take positions that are con-
trary to popular trends in the field of race relations.

"Racism" versus "Diversity"

One example is found in the Institutes' use of the term "racism." There is a
growing movement among race relations consultants and firms to avoid
using the word "racism" in their efforts to eradicate racism from corporations, college campuses, and governmental agencies. They prefer to use the
term "diversity" because it is less threatening to most Whites and to many
people of color who are prospering economically and don't want to be reminded of the bitter past. "Why rip the scab off deep wounds?" these people
ask.

We feel this insistence on using the term "diversity" is a way of avoiding
and denying reality, for the racial wounds have not healed. Focusing on
"diversity" gives the impression that racism is not as virulent as it was before

the civil rights movement of the 1960s and suggests that all one has to do to tranquilize a tense, racially divided community is devise means to tolerate one another and respect one another's culture. This rejection of reality can lead to trouble for individuals, the community, and institutions. When racist acts are encountered, those who have been focusing on diversity and toleration are not emotionally or intellectually prepared to deal with it. This lack of preparedness supports the continuation of painful internal and external conflicts in our society. Though these racial conflicts aren't as volatile today as they have been in the past, this is true only because we have become more skillful at concealing race-related pain, fear, anger, hatred, and suspicion. A lot of creative energy is going into pretense and self- and group-deception. But there are limits to how long a person or a community can control a growing accumulation of negative emotional energy.

To overcome racism it is essential to understand exactly what it is, how it was conceived, and how it has grown and spread as a divisive social force, permeating every city, town, village, and home in our country. When diversity is emphasized there is a tendency to avoid probing the nature of racism; instead, considerable energy is expended in mastering the art of political correctness. As a consequence, the treatment employed to produce racial harmony is, at best, superficial. To remedy the disease of racism successfully, an accurate diagnosis is required. Otherwise the resulting treatments merely perform racial "face-lifts" instead of the surgery needed to remove the cancer from an ailing body that refuses to acknowledge its malady.

Facing the Disease Head-On

While the Institutes for the Healing of Racism approach racism head-on, the approach is non-confrontational, safe, and non-threatening. Facing reality is the first step to healing.

As they have explored the nature of racism, the Institutes for the Healing of Racism have discovered that it is a disease. Certainly it is not a bacterial or viral infection, nor an organic defect. It is, however, a psychological, emotional, and spiritual disorder that can set off physical ailments such as hypertension, heart disease, and strokes, especially among those who are the traditional targets of racism. The medical establishment recognizes, and it is a well-known fact, that attitudes and feelings can seriously disturb physical health and functioning.

In proclaiming that racism is a disease, the Institutes have received some criticism. The fact that the medical establishment has not labeled racism as a disease is the most common criticism voiced by our critics. We counter that argument by pointing out that it took many years before the American Medical Association acknowledged alcoholism as a disease. Yet the criticism continues, even after the pathology of the disease is fully explained and backed up with scientific proofs. We have found that possessing a Ph.D. is no safeguard against prejudice toward our findings. Some of the most energetic critics can be found in academia.

In 1967 there were a number of psychiatrists who were openly proclaiming that racism was a public health hazard. Among them were Dr. Alvin Poiussant of Harvard and Dr. Price Cobb, the author of *Black Rage.* Their proclamation caught the attention of Senator Fred Harris, who was chairing a Senate subcommittee exploring the state of children's mental health. Convinced that these psychiatrists were making sense, Senator Harris asked them to establish a task force to produce a position paper proving that racism is, indeed, an infectious public hazard.

After the position paper was produced, Senator Harris asked the task force to present its paper before his subcommittee. While the evidence that was presented was convincing, every Senator except Senator Harris declared that the American people were not ready to hear what the paper reported, and they shelved it.

The Institutes for the Healing of Racism believe that now is the time to hear the evidence. We believe this for two reasons: One, because it is the truth. While it is difficult to let go of falsehoods that we have been conditioned to believe are truths, in the end, acceptance of the truth has a purifying effect on individuals and communities. Besides, we are told by a fairly reliable source that "the truth shall make you free." The second reason is that knowing the truth puts us in a better position to create a remedy that will heal the disease and not simply mask its symptoms, as so many present-day "remedies" do. Again, without a proper diagnosis, the treatment that is prescribed usually exacerbates the malady.

All Americans are affected by racism in varying degrees because we live in a fundamentally racist society. There isn't a region, area, district, or hamlet that is free of it. This doesn't mean that America is patently evil. As we have already mentioned, there is much that is good about North America. But we do have shortcomings, and racism is arguably the most dehumanizing of them. It has been thwarting our nations' development, eroding their very souls for more than two centuries. Their national leaders' unawareness of the degenerative process that is at work has been compounding the problem.

Once cured of the disease of racism, the United States and Canada would be universally acknowledged as truly the lands of the free, which today is more of a slogan than a reality. There are a large number of North Americans who know in their hearts that they are not fully free. For them the chain of slavery hasn't been removed, only extended. They sense this every time they enter a White-owned restaurant, every time they shop in a department store in a White neighborhood, every time they look into their car's rearview mirror and see a police car trailing them.

Who Is Affected

Because America is fundamentally a racist society, all Americans are affected by racism to some degree. There are some Whites who would vigorously protest such a sweeping indictment and proclaim with complete sincerity that they are free of racial prejudice. This is wishful thinking on their part. Many well-meaning White people who openly oppose racism and can cite wonderful things that they have done for America's downtrodden and oppressed think they are free of racism.

However, the reality is that no one living in America can escape the poisonous tentacles of racism, including even those people who are the traditional targets of racism. Why is this so? Because racism is a powerful element of the American culture; it is part of our collective consciousness, and it is deeply rooted in our hearts. A thorough and unedited study of how racism came into being in North America and of how it was perpetuated for centuries by the most powerful colonial and federal leaders and institutions will give you some idea why it is practically impossible to live in this country all of your life without being affected by racism. We pick it up by osmosis. Sadly, we don't have a choice in the matter—even those of us who are the most philanthropic and the most human rights-conscious.

Racism is so pervasive that when immigrants come to America they, too, are infected by the disease of racism eventually. If they are persons of color, they eventually find themselves slotted in a place reserved for Americans of color. They are forced either to learn how to cope with the monster of racism or to be devoured by it. For Whites it is not a matter of consciously choosing to view African Americans, American Indians, Hispanics, and Asians as inferior. It is unconsciously adopting the view of the most powerful political and economic elements in the land, elements who may even be doing good works to foster racial harmony through a benign, patronizing "White man's burden" approach. The fact that "affirmative action" programs exist is a sign that racial equality does not yet exist in America. A close look at the American landscape will reveal that, proportionately, minorities are much poorer than Whites. For centuries they have been denied the opportunities to advance socially and economically that Whites have had. As a result, in places like the Ogala Sioux Pine Ridge reservation in South Dakota, 75 percent of adults are unemployed. Hopelessness, frustration, and anger are rampant in most other American-Indian reservations as well. Alcoholism and suicide are chronic problems. The same is true of the hundreds of African-American ghettoes found in every part of America. Though racially segregated schools were declared unconstitutional by the U.S. Supreme Court in 1952, 70 percent of Hispanic children attend segregated schools, and more than 66 percent of African-American children have never seen a White student in their classroom. In many communities, the busing of African-American children to White schools has turned out to be counterproductive because White teachers and students aren't psychologically prepared to wholeheartedly accept the African-American students as their equals. Most of the African-American students end up being emotionally traumatized, placed in lower learning tracks and feeling isolated from the mainstream of students. The so-called solutions to racism that have been prescribed by well-meaning governmental and private agencies have not taken into account the true nature of the problem. Consequently little meaningful progress has been made toward uprooting and eliminating racism in America. A change of heart, not the mastering of political correctness, is what is needed.

All Whites suffer from an inherent and at times subconscious sense of superiority toward people of color. Notice that we are not qualifying the number of Whites. We mean *all* Whites. We are not saying that Whites are born with a racist gene. They have been conditioned to feel superior, and the conditioning is part of a legacy dating back to the 1500s, when the first European settlers arrived in North America. Because their political and religious leaders felt that American Indians and Africans were savages and lower beings, the rank-and-file Whites adopted the same attitude. Schools, churches, and governmental institutions reflected the attitude. This attitude was passed on from generation to generation and from White-ruled colony to colony, eventually influencing the thinking of the Founding Fathers, the framers of the U.S. Constitution. It was practically impossible to avoid being influenced by the aura of White supremacy brought to America's shores by the early European settlers. Not even the abolitionist movement, the Civil War, the freeing of four million slaves, and the Reconstruction campaign that followed, nor even the civil rights laws of the 1960s or affirmative action legislation have been able to change the sense of superiority that White Americans feel in relation to their fellow citizens of color.

This attitude, in time, has become institutionalized, ingrained in the American way of life as an obsession, which is an irrational, fixed idea or set of feelings. It is irrational because it is based on the erroneous belief that Whites are inherently superior to everyone else. This racial obsession is another term for prejudice, which is an unquestioned emotional attachment to a falsehood that is assumed to be the truth. In other words, it is an emotional commitment to ignorance. (For a historical overview of how this attitude developed and grew, see the books *Racism: Unraveling the Fear* and *Coming of Age at the Millennium: Embracing the Oneness of Humankind,* by Nathan Rutstein.)

White people today did not choose to take on this obsession. It is a social inheritance that we have accepted unconsciously, much as we accept, without thinking, a custom that everyone around us, including those we admire most, practices and never questions. It is important to note that possessing this racial obsession does not automatically make a person evil. While there are racial bigots who commit hate crimes, there are many well-meaning people—human-rights advocates, members of the clergy, teachers—who are unaware that they have the obsession.

However, out of the need to survive, people of color have learned to detect it even among the most well-meaning Whites, whose sense of superiority is usually manifested through unconscious condescending or patronizing behavior. Though such patronizing attitudes and behavior on the part of Whites are not as dramatic as blowing up an African-American church or a synagogue, they do more harm in the long run. Collectively, the well-meaning Whites' patronizing manner creates an inhospitable atmosphere for people of color. It is like an invisible, odorless gas that cripples them little by little by reinforcing feelings of inferiority, lack of confidence, and self-hatred. That is why many African Americans and Hispanics avoid as much as possible frequenting White-dominated places. While there are laws against hate crimes, there are no laws that prohibit anyone from exhibiting feelings of superiority toward people of color. In fact, many governmental agencies that are supposed to protect minorities' rights are staffed by people of good will who are unaware of their own prejudices and unwittingly offend those they are trying to help. As a result, many who need the help never return to ask for it. It is often a matter of pride as well as protection against humiliation.

Because of the way they are treated by Whites, there is a grassroots movement among African Americans toward separatism. They want to avoid the inhospitable atmosphere as much as possible, for it is too painful to endure. They know that the likelihood of changing the atmosphere are slim, for the Whites who possess most of the power in America are comfortable with it. They also know that many of the Whites who unwittingly reinforce the inhospitable atmosphere are people of influence such as lawyers, doctors, teachers, professors, clergy, industrialists, and legislators who are too set in their ways to change. Unaware of their subtle racism, they see and feel no need to change. Thus many people of color who are the targets of racism are reluctant to confront the perpetrators for fear of alienating or insulting people who have the power to sabotage their careers or deprive them of mortgages. There is also a fatigue factor: It takes so much energy to fight for your rights, and in the end the Whites always find a way to win the battle. To preserve some semblance of psychological equilibrium, many African Americans avoid as much as possible interactions with Whites. That's why after work hours, most African Americans retreat to African-American enclaves, where they can find some relief from the pressures of being African-American in a White-dominated community.

Most Whites usually manifest their racism compulsively. For example, when driving through an African-American neighborhood they will quickly roll up the windows of their car and lock the doors. This is a conditioned reflex, often done without thinking. Such behavior is a sign that they are suffering from a form of obsessive-compulsive disorder known as racial prejudice. This disorder is not easily cured, mainly because those who suffer from it refuse to acknowledge that they are afflicted by it.

The Difficulty of Addressing the Problem

Earlier, racial prejudice was defined as an emotional attachment to igno-rance. We have found that it is actually more difficult for individuals to overcome the emotional attachment to the ignorance than to overcome the ignorance itself. Overcoming the attachment to ignorance requires unravel-ing a tightly woven, multilayered obsession that has deep roots stemming back to the 1500s. This undertaking is a monumental challenge, for it in-volves tackling the fear of discovering that certain "sacred" beliefs are actu-ally falsehoods. Disillusionment can be awfully painful, especially if you have nothing to replace the beliefs that you have always held sacred—such as the belief that Christopher Columbus discovered America, or that the Puritans began the process of civilizing the American "wilderness," that George Washington never lied, or that Abraham Lincoln's great love for African Americans was why he freed the slaves. To avoid such emotional trauma, individuals commonly refuse to take up the challenge and instead continue, along with everyone else, to cling to the sacred beliefs while turn-ing a deaf ear to all attempts to examine the validity of their beliefs.

Defusing the emotional attachment to ignorance requires a much greater effort than overcoming simple ignorance. After all, a lifetime of condition-ing has gone into developing the emotional attachment. To illustrate the difficulty, take, for example, Americans' reverence for Christopher Colum-bus, who is hailed as the discoverer of their land. Statues of the explorer dot the American landscape. Cities have been named after him. A federal holi-day has been established to honor his exploits. True, the national venera-tion of Columbus started long before the true nature of his exploits in the Western Hemisphere became common knowledge. Today, however, it can certainly be argued that his actions were those of a racist mass murderer.

Through Columbus's command, more than 120,000 Arawak Indians were killed, and thousands of others were enslaved and tortured. Many committed suicide, and many mothers killed their infants rather than allow them to endure what was certain to be a lifetime of slavery and torture. A popular punishment carried out by Columbus's men was to cut off the hands of those slaves who did not meet their work quota.

Though history has recorded the many atrocities Columbus committed when he came to the "New World" looking for gold, we continue to revere him. We don't want to hear the truth. We don't want to know the truth. We cling tenaciously to the myth of Christopher Columbus, which we have been taught is the truth. Any attempt to dislodge the myth is vigorously resisted. So we continue to think of a racist mass murderer as the discoverer of America, continue to march in Columbus Day parades, and continue to teach our children the Columbus myth.

It does not seem to matter to the great majority of Americans and Canadians that we are perpetuating a falsehood. Many of us, especially our political and educational leadership, now know what Columbus really did, yet we do not allow that knowledge to change our feelings about a national hero who committed heinous crimes against his fellow human beings. In reality, this is more than strange thinking and behavior, more than a gross injustice. It is unrecognized insanity. The great majority of Americans do not recognize it as such because, for the most part, they harbor the same feelings about Columbus. The rationalization is, "If others feel the way I do, then what I believe can't be bad. Besides, it's a fun tradition, what with the parades and pageants and things."

A more rational and honest response to the facts would be to dismantle the statues, rename the cities, and discontinue the Columbus Day holiday and all of its associated festivities. But there is no real desire to make the changes. Highly educated White adults occupying powerful posts refuse even to consider the idea of change.

Despite the difficulty of loosening the emotional attachment to falsehood and ignorance, it is indeed possible to dismantle the attachment. In most cases a sensitive, gradual process of chipping away is required.

Exposure to a considerable amount of patience, sustained love, and knowledge are necessary for a person to change beliefs that, through the years, have provided a sense of security and comfort. Challenging one's belief system usually provokes resistance because there is a natural desire to protect what makes one feel comfortable and secure. If the challenge is forceful, arguments and even fights can result, and feuds may develop. Ideally, the challenge should be offered with love. Truth that is conveyed in an attitude of patient and unqualified love can penetrate even the hardest of hearts. This is what most participants experience in sessions of the Institutes for the Healing of Racism.

Internalized Racism

People of color in America are affected differently by the disease of racism than Whites are. Most people of color suffer, in varying degrees, from internalized racism. The characteristics of internalized racism can be seen in a lack of confidence, low self-esteem, and not liking oneself because of one's skin-color. These characteristics stem from an inherent sense of inferiority that has nothing to do with one's native intelligence or creative capacity and ability. Those who suffer from internalized racism are victims of oppression.

The oppression has taken many forms over the centuries. During the days of slavery it took the form of carefully conceived terrorist tactics such as flogging or the mere threat of flogging for acts of insubordination. At times it took the form of forceful indoctrination through the recitation of a slave catechism, which powerfully reinforced the alleged inferiority of people of color. Unfortunately, the reinforcement continued after slavery was abolished. How did it continue? The physical abolition of slavery did not change the racial attitude of Whites institutions and society; all of the old attitudes have persisted. As a result, people of color have been continually reminded of their low station in society, and they have continued to struggle against invisible barriers that prevent them from being what they want to be. Americans of color have been conditioned to "know their place." Fear of physical and emotional harm to themselves and their families has kept them there.

The slights and subtle humiliations that African Americans receive from their White acquaintances and coworkers are commonplace. Sociologist Joe Feagin relates the story of an eighty-two-year-old scientist who kept count of the times he was racially slighted. Starting at the age of twenty, he figured that he was slighted about two hundred and fifty times a year. In his lifetime, he said, he had been the target of more than fifteen thousand known racial slights. "That," the elderly man added, "wears you down."

The famous tennis player Arthur Ashe felt that being a person of color in America was a heavy burden. By all accounts he was a man who had "made it" in the world. Not only was he a great tennis player, he was a humanitarian, a civil rights worker, a wonderful father and husband, a successful business man, the recipient of many awards. This mild-mannered man contracted AIDS through a blood transfusion while undergoing heart surgery. Shortly before he passed away, his memoir titled *Days of Grace* was released. In it he bared his soul and commented on what it was like to be a person of color in his native land: "Being an African-American in America was far more difficult to endure than having AIDS." In light of this observation, it is important to think about what life in America must be like for those African Americans who don't enjoy the fame and fortune of Arthur Ashe.

Some African Americans and American Indians who are plagued by internalized racism find themselves the victims of post-traumatic stress disorder (PTSD), which can have serious physical consequences such as hypertension, heart disease, and stroke.* Many PTSD sufferers turn to drugs and alcohol to escape from the haunting symptoms of the psychological malady.

Any person of color in America who wants to be fully free must face and deal with the very real problem of internalized racism. Freedom is more than being able to vote and attend the movie of your choice, and it is more than living in a predominantly White middle-class suburban neighborhood. It means being internally free—in other words, no longer being haunted by feelings of inferiority because of your skin color, no longer being willing to remain in a social place prescribed by the dominant culture, and finally letting go of anger and rage. The completely free African American has purged himself or herself of the effects of some four hundred years of White brainwashing. Though it can be done, it is not an easy task. The biggest obstacle is the resistance on the part of many influential, well-to-do African Americans to accept the reality of internalized racism. They have forced themselves and others to believe it doesn't exist. Sadly, doing so only prolongs the struggle to become fully free.

The Institutes for the Healing of Racism provide a pathway to complete freedom, not only for African Americans, Hispanics, Asians, and Ameri-

---

* A PTSD sufferer who suppresses that which is unbearable to the conscious mind is trying to ignore it, trying to pretend it isn't there. In time, and without treatment, it will destroy the person, just as any illness left untreated eventually cripples and kills the body.

can Indians, but also for Whites. Whites will find full freedom only when they have purged themselves of the falsehood that, because of their skin color, they are inherently superior to people of a different skin color.

The Problem of Denial

Denial is the greatest obstacle to finding full freedom, but it is not only a White issue; people of color suffer from it too. Earlier denial was described as a carefully concealed mental maneuver that springs from a sense of shame. When you are ashamed of a thought or feeling, you repress it and convince yourself that you don't really think or feel that way.

It is understandable that White people of good will would be ashamed of having negative feelings toward a person of different skin color. It is equally understandable that African Americans and other minorities would be ashamed of having sudden feelings of inferiority. While these are very natural human emotional reflexes, they are not honest reflexes. Unless the true underlying racial feelings are addressed and overcome, the unaware oppressor and the oppressed will continue to feel uneasy in interracial encounters. The unconscious mind is an important part of us because it is where our true feelings fester. In essence it is the concealed "true self." It influences the development of our personality and the way we really feel. The conscious mind is the cover-up of an African-American person's anger and bitterness, and it is the cover-up of a White person's negative racial feelings and attitudes of racial superiority. Freeing oneself of whatever is festering in the unconscious has physical health benefits. Prolonged pretense causes chronic stress, which can set off psychosomatic pain as well as high blood pressure, the forerunner of heart attacks and strokes.

It takes courage to acknowledge your racism and to be willing to engage in a healing process that will eventually free you of negative racial feelings or a sense of inferiority and inadequacy. Thelma Khelgati was one such person. Though Thelma was the director of graduate studies at a college in Massachusetts and had traveled widely throughout the world, she recognized that she was a victim of internalized racism. She was somewhat shocked to discover it, for she mingled freely, and with some degree of self-assurance, wherever she lived and worked. Her marriage to a prominent White man seemed to make her acceptable in most quarters. She was so busy pursuing a successful career and running a secure and healthy home that she didn't have time to think about her internalized racism.

But she was infected, all right, and that realization dawned in the most unlikely place—a duplicating center in Cambridge, Massachusetts. Wanting a perfect photocopy of an important report she and her husband had written, she took her manuscript to what she had heard was one of the best duplicating centers in town.

When she stepped into the center, she thought she was in the wrong place. All of the personnel, including the owner, were African American. Her immediate impulse was to leave because her gut feeling was "These people are incapable of the kind of job I want done." It didn't matter that she herself was African American, that as a college youth she had been a member of a Black power organization that had preached separatism.

Because the shop was in Cambridge, the site of Harvard University, she had assumed that White people would be operating it, people she would feel had the expertise to do what she wanted done. Thelma didn't leave. She stood near the entrance in sort of a trance for a few moments, stunned that she, a college-educated African-American woman, could feel that way toward other African Americans. There was nothing she could do to overcome the feeling.

In some ways, that sense of helplessness to rid oneself of something one knows is wrong is worse than the infection itself. You can have a Ph.D. and hold an important public post and still be infected by internalized racism. This became apparent when Dr. Franklyn Jennifer came to Springfield Technical Community College to bid farewell to the faculty and administration. He was retiring as chancellor of the Massachusetts Board of Regents of Higher Education to become president of his alma mater, Howard University, a predominantly African-American institution.

Dr. Jennifer spoke from the heart. He appealed to the professors to make a concerted effort to help African-American students overcome their lack of self-esteem, their sense of inferiority. Using himself as an example, he demonstrated how internalized racism affects a person.

He shared with the audience an incident that had occurred shortly before he came to Springfield. A distinguished academic organization had asked him to address a conference in Philadelphia. When he and his party arrived at the airport, they were told that the major airlines weren't flying to Philadelphia because of inclement weather. Only a commuter airline, located in a different terminal, was flying. After a short fifteen-minute wait, the pilot showed up. Dr. Jennifer's immediate reaction was not to board the small propeller-driven plane because the pilot was African American. He wanted a White person in the pilot's seat, especially since the weather was bad. He knew it was wrong to feel that way, but that feeling was real, and there was nothing he could do to overcome it. It didn't matter that he was a Ph.D., a noted microbiologist and the head of the state colleges and universities in Massachusetts. He was unable to rid himself of that feeling that had been a part of him since he was a child.

Most African-American children are not immune to internalized racism. Drs. Mamie and Kenneth Clark, psychologists, found that out in a telling 1950s psychological study they organized. They tested three- to seven-year-old African-American children in several American cities, in both the North and South, to determine how extensive the effects of internalized racism were. They ushered them into a room with a display of dark-skinned dolls and light-skinned dolls. The children were told, Give me the doll you like best, Give me the nice doll, Give me the doll that looks bad, and Give me the doll that is the nice color. The great majority of the children preferred the White dolls.

Nearly forty years later, after the African-American community had been exposed to many "Black Is Beautiful" campaigns, the test was redone—with no change in the results. Constant exposure to positive advertising campaigns can't erase what is continuously and unwittingly reinforced at home, in school, and in society in general.

The Institutes for the Healing of Racism are not a quick fix. Participants are engaged in a step-by-step process, but the progress they make keeps them coming back. Cleansing the heart of the poison of prejudice and cleansing the heart of the psychologically wounding effects of prejudice on those who are its object occurs in stages. Whatever negative beliefs and attitudes are shed lighten the burden. Because participants can sense the advancement being made, they are motivated to keep treading the pathway. Liking the feeling, they happily sense that it will only intensify when more "shedding" takes place. Consequently they look forward to continued wholehearted participation in the Institutes. The more progress is made, the more certain the participants become that they will eventually experience full freedom.

A MOVEMENT OF HOPE
AND OPTIMISM

Much effort and money is being funneled into North American programs to create and maintain a tranquil social climate on college campuses and in corporations and governmental agencies. The emphasis is on nonviolent containment, not change. This approach is employed because most of those who are trying to create such a condition believe that as long as humans exist there will always be racism. To prove their point, they refer to humanity's bloody history. They believe that lording over others is part of human nature and that what was done in the past will inevitably be repeated in the present and future. Thus they channel their energy into trying to keep the problem from erupting into rioting, bodily harm, or hate crimes. Academics who subscribe to this view call this tactic "managing racism." It is growing in popularity because more and more people who promote it feel there is no alternative.

The Institutes for the Healing of Racism have a different, far more hopeful view. They believe that human beings have the potential of doing wonderful things, as history has already revealed, and that people are capable of changing attitudes and behavior, even sometimes attaining a saintly condition. All human beings have the potential to become like Mother Teresa or Martin Luther King, Jr.

We believe that attempting to solve the problem of racism by "managing" it or through "diversity management" is an expression of hopelessness. Furthermore, we believe that such approaches are painful, anxiety-producing exercises that, in the end, prolong the racial problem, for they detract attention from the healing process that is essential to overcoming racism and healing human hearts.

Faking race unity or forcing it upon a community won't work. Trying to organize an atmosphere of racial tolerance without addressing the underlying causes of racism generates considerable tension among those trying to carry out their objective. In most cases those responsible for organizing such projects are people of good will who are trying hard to hide their own racial prejudice.

In time, however, the bubble of pretense bursts. That usually happens in one of two ways: The energy required to maintain a prejudice-free facade eventually dissipates, leaving us emotionally drained. We usually retreat to environments where there is little chance of having interracial encounters and where there is enough time to shore up the rationalizations that support our denial. Reinvigorated after such a period of rest, we may reenter the torture chamber of pretense—if we're committed to the cause of breaking down racial barriers. This routine can go on for some time, ultimately accomplishing very little toward creating the tranquil social climate that is the goal. In the end, our commitment to overcoming racism wanes under the mounting pressure of keeping up the pretense. If we are activists at heart, we will channel our energies into other causes such as "Save the Whale" campaigns or environmentalism.

Being rebuked by a minority person for displaying a patronizing attitude is another reason for dropping out of the anti-racism struggle. Usually when we are challenged we are so full of denial that we can't appreciate the fact that we're being exposed to the truth, that we are infected with the disease of racism, and that if we consent to healing ourselves, we would become more liberated. To overcome our hurt feelings, we may rationalize the experience, convincing ourselves that we were insulted by an African American or Hispanic or American Indian who hates White people. If we don't drop out, we'll seek out the more insecure minority people who are prone to stroke White people's egos. In this case, we may choose to become engaged in a conscience-satisfying race-relations effort that generates lots of motion but no meaningful advancement in the field of race relations—something like an annual multicultural arts festival, a race unity picnic, a community-wide Martin Luther King, Jr., birthday celebration, a sports event that brings together colleagues of various races.

The point is that race-relations projects whose primary aim is to promote tolerance are not going to eradicate the racism that has infected human hearts. Tolerance, after all, is a fragile emotional condition. It curtails prejudicial behavior without getting rid of the prejudice. The prejudice remains deactivated, but it is still present and can easily be reactivated by a rumor, an irrational remark, or an offensive act.

Tolerance has its place. It should be seen as a stepping-stone to love and unity. Unfortunately most diversity programs don't share that perspective. For the most part, diversity workers view creating a tolerant atmosphere as the ultimate goal. The trouble is that people would rather be loved than tolerated. The preference for love rather than mere tolerance is real because, we believe, humans were created to love and to be loved. Human beings are endowed with a boundless capacity for love. When we are unaware of this capacity, we don't experience it in our interactions with others. This makes it difficult for us to love anyone; the most we can do is to express tolerance.

In the Institutes for the Healing of Racism, participants discover their capacity to love and learn to develop it. Obviously when we refer to love we do not have in mind the kind of affection portrayed in television soap operas or paperback romance novels. The love we refer to is essentially a spiritual force whereby two people are drawn to one another and unity is established.

Since you cannot love someone you don't know, knowledge is required before love can bloom. Of course there's always the danger of mistaking infatuation with love. Infatuation is based on superficial or distorted knowledge. True love results from really knowing a person and becoming aware of his or her real interior condition and positive characteristics. This is the kind of love that results in true lifelong friendship.

Dialogue of the Spirit

Through a dialogue of the spirit, people really get to know one another. In time they learn to appreciate each other, they are attracted to one another, and their hearts are bonded. When this happens, the love process, which is cyclical in nature, starts: The more you know the one you love, the stronger your love becomes. Therefore true lovers continually seek more knowledge of one another. One of the ways knowledge is gained is through honest communication, and this is usually achieved when participants in the Institutes for the Healing of Racism become involved in the dialogue of the spirit.

Before describing the dialogue, it is important to point out that it is unlike the conventional dialogue in which people exchange views—often deeply entrenched views. Most of the time such exchanges happen between individuals who don't really know each other. Whatever is known may be based on superficial encounters or hearsay. This widely practiced form of dialoguing usually generates more heat than light. For the most part, such discussions end up as debates or clashes of ego that turn into arguments and perhaps even power struggles. They become the spawning place for resentment, hatred, and jealousy. On many college and university campuses those who have similar beliefs usually unite and clash with cliques that hold opposing views. In this fractured academic atmosphere, backbiting, character assassination, and cutthroat political maneuvering are commonplace. It certainly doesn't generate trust among the dialoguing factions.

In contrast, the dialogue of the spirit aims at generating trust between participants in the dialogue. Once trust is established an open and healthy exchange of views can occur, often producing constructive results. People who care about each other will usually take to heart what the other person says, even when there is some disagreement.

There are three phases to the dialogue of the spirit. Phase 1 is a five-minute meditation in which the participant focuses on a question offered by the facilitator. The question is based on an aspect from one of three themes: (1) the oneness of humankind, (2) the origins of racism in our country, (3) the pathology of racism and how it affects us.

To help participants gain a truer understanding of their racial conditioning, they are asked to zero in on the images that come to mind and the positive and negative emotions that are generated within while meditating on the question. Participants are encouraged to link the emotions and images to personal experiences or true stories experienced by others close to them. By doing this exercise over a period of time, a person can eventually break out of the hard shell of denial. Facing and accepting the truth is the most important step toward winning freedom from the stranglehold of race prejudice or internalized racism. To try to achieve the same end without taking that crucial step will only reinforce a falsehood that is assumed to be the truth. Although other race relations activities may give us the feeling that we are doing something to overcome racism, in the end the effort will prove fruitless in terms of healing our own infection or wound of racism.

After the meditation, the group breaks into pairs. Each person is given five minutes to relate the images that came to mind and the emotions that were generated within during the meditation. This is strictly a sharing and listening exercise. It is not a conversation, consultation, or an exchange of views. The sharer doesn't offer opinions, analysis, or commentary, but shares the images that came to mind and the accompanying emotions. By staying focused we learn something about ourselves that perhaps we weren't aware of. Sincere seekers of truth and open-minded people generally welcome such self-knowledge.

Those who are listening do not utter a word and refrain from judging, analyzing, or evaluating the person who is sharing. They do not take what is being said personally, realizing that this is a safeguard against becoming defensive. They concentrate on what the sharer is saying, trying to sense the sharer's feelings by focusing on what the individual is saying and how it is being shared. In other words, they are listening with the heart. By doing this time and time again, participants develop their capacity to sense the reality of others and penetrate their façade, getting to know their real feelings and, in some cases, even the thoughts behind the words. In time the listener becomes more compassionate and empathetic not only with other participants but with everyone they encounter.

In most North American societies listening is a lost art. The emphasis in conversation, for the most part, is on getting one's point across, attaining the upper hand in the discussion. Most discussions end up becoming a debate with a winner and a loser. Very little effort is put into listening with the heart. In fact, listening with the heart is classified by many men and women as some strange exercise bordering on the occult. Our poor listening skills and our rejection of intuitive learning have led to growing suspicion, fear, and distrust among people. Because we don't really know each other—and this is true even among married couples—there is no real love between us.

By being an active and supportive listener, we convey to the sharer that we care for and respect them. We develop trust. When that happens, the person who is sharing is inspired to dig deeper into their unconscious and reveal more than they originally thought they were capable of revealing. This cathartic experience is the beginning of the journey to full freedom. By learning things about one another that we never knew before, we are drawn emotionally closer. When we are sharing, the fact that we were really listened to draws us closer to those who have listened to us. Love develops, leading in time to the unity of two souls.

When we listen we don't utter a word, though we may be moved to reach out and grasp the hands of the person who is sharing, especially when they are having difficulty sharing all that they want to reveal. Holding hands can send a heartfelt nonverbal message to the sharer. The message is "I'm with you. I appreciate what you are saying. I know you want to say more, and I feel that you are capable of getting it out. I'm with you all the way." That gesture of encouragement reinforces the trust that is being established between both parties.

It has been our experience that holding hands usually inspires sharers to reveal things they thought they could never reveal. They become grateful for the expression of love and confidence and happy that they have been able to overcome the difficulty. As bonding occurs, participants learn that much wisdom can be expressed without uttering a word.

After five minutes of sharing, the sharer and listener reverse roles.

When the one-on-one sharing is completed, the participants gather in a circle to engage in further sharing on a voluntary basis. Before the facilitator poses the same question to the group, the guidelines for group sharing are read aloud.

They are as follows:

1. Sharing is voluntary

2. We want to create a safe, loving, and respectful atmosphere.

3. Sharing is about one's own feelings, experiences, perceptions, etc.

4. We are not always going to agree or see everything the same way, and that's OK.

5. Each person has the right to, and responsibility for, his or her own feelings, thoughts, and beliefs.

6. It is important to avoid criticism or judgment of other people, their points-of-view, and their feelings.

7. Avoid getting tied up in debate and argument. It rarely changes anything or anyone and ultimately tends to inhibit sharing.

8. We can only change ourselves. Our change and growth may, however, inspire someone else.

9. Refrain from singling out any individual as "representing" his or her group or issue.

10. It is important to give full attention to whomever is talking.

11. Feelings are important.

12. We will surely make mistakes in our efforts, but mistakes are occasions for learning and forgiving.

13. We came together to try to learn about the disease of racism and to promote a healing process.
14. We may laugh and cry together, share pain, joy, fear, and anger.
15. We hope we will leave these meetings with a deeper understanding and a renewed hope for the future of humanity.

These guidelines for sharing are read aloud at every group session. Though it may seem unnecessarily repetitive, we think it is necessary to overcome some of our bad interpersonal communications habits such as interrupting speakers, pontificating, preaching, becoming defensive or argumentative, giving unsolicited advice. By internalizing the guidelines we become effective listeners with the heart. We are forced to redirect our attention from ourselves to the person who is sharing. At first it may not be evident that by listening with the heart we learn to be less self-centered and more concerned with others. After a number of sessions, however, participants find themselves focusing primarily on the sharer and enjoying freedom from the demands of ego. They gain a new appreciation for service, for they realize that wholehearted listening is a life-enriching service for the listener as well as for the sharer. While the listener gains satisfaction in knowing that being a willing, sincere sounding board for another human being helps them to heal, the sharer gives the listener an opportunity to discover and express compassion. Both parties find themselves less materially centered and more spiritually focused. When most of the participants are in that frame of mind, a collective spirit of love grows within the room. It is so appealing that people don't want to leave. This is understandable, because they have discovered a life-changing reality they had not known before, a reality of which most other people are unaware.

The dialogue-of-the-spirit process proves to the open-minded that we all have the potential to change our attitudes and behavior, that we can go beyond nonviolent containment in dealing with racial issues, that it is possible to transform ourselves and our communities. Just think of what could happen to a community if the majority of inhabitants derived the spiritual benefits the sharer and listener derive from engaging in the dialogue of the spirit. (For a step-by-step description of the dialogue of the spirit format, see the appendix.)

TRANSFORMATION

Most individuals and institutions involved in race relations work are seeking solutions to the problem of racism. Even those who are involved in "managing racism" or "diversity training" are attempting to solve the problem.

At this point in their evolution the Institutes for the Healing of Racism are not concerned with searching for a solution to the problem of racism. Our primary focus is on the transformation of individuals, for without such transformation, we believe, there can be no solution. We believe that the solution to the racial problem is inherent in individual racial transformation. A racially transformed person is no longer afflicted by the disease of racism. A collection of racially transformed men and women becomes a force for love and harmony in the community. When the number of such people increases, the journey to a solution is shortened.

It isn't enough to be involved in an anti-racism campaign. Anti-racism is a negative approach, and negative approaches do not produce positive results. You don't fight fire with fire. Those involved in anti-racism campaigns who feel they have overcome their own racism are fooling themselves. We have found that those who believe they have gotten rid of their racism without replacing it with a genuine belief in the oneness of humankind only experience temporary remission of the disease. For true racial transformation to occur, a person must overcome their negative racial feelings and replace them with a genuine belief in the oneness of humankind.

All of the effort and money channeled into diversity training has produced negligible results. In fact, we are not aware of any substantial impact. Diversity training has not removed from many White people's marrow the poison of racial prejudice and feelings of superiority. It hasn't overcome the internalized racism that plagues so many racial minorities. What it has done is to create the impression that significant advancements have been made in overcoming racism. Much energy has been expended to convince themselves and society that the illusion of race-relations progress that they have woven is, indeed, reality. To attempt to solve the racial problem without experiencing transformation is like participating in an archery contest and trying to hit the target without an arrow.

There are three phases to transformational process of the Institutes for the Healing of Racism. In the first phase participants learn to identify their racial infection or wound, becoming aware of their true racial conditioning. If they have been in denial, they break out of it and find themselves facing reality. This can be painful, but the fact that there are other participants in the same circumstance lessens the pain. When facilitators commiserate with them and explain that knowing their real racial conditioning enables them to begin the journey to healing, the pain usually subsides. The facilitators' compassionate reaction to the pain is believable because they have experienced it themselves. Sharing their experiences with the participants is a source of encouragement to newcomers. Instead of fleeing, participants persevere with a degree of safe curiosity, if not hope.

In the second phase the healing process accelerates as participants engage in the dialogue of the spirit. The more they engage in this experience, the more progress they make in their healing.

The third phase is intertwined with the second phase. While participants purge themselves of the poison of racial prejudice or internalized racism they are exposed to the realities underlying the principle of the oneness of humankind. They take part in a replacement exercise, for while they are getting rid of the poison of prejudice and internalized racism, they are internalizing the reality of the oneness of humankind. How this is done will be explained in a later chapter.

Participants who go through a ten-week program of weekly two-hour sessions find themselves a lot freer than before. Because they are no longer in denial there is no need to engage in tension-producing pretense. They are no longer captives of the prevailing fractured view of humanity that has caused so much misunderstanding and friction throughout the ages. As genuine believers in the oneness of humankind, they look upon everyone they encounter as a member of their family. It doesn't matter how they are dressed, the type of work they do, what language they speak, the color of their skin, their religion, ethnicity, or culture. The often-used term "children of God" suddenly takes on a profound meaning and no longer seems like a platitude or cliché. God is seen to be the super-parent of all six billion human beings on our planet, making everyone family members. The blindfold created by a deluded society has been removed.

When a great majority of people have experienced this kind of transformation there will be no need to seek a solution to racism, for the fruit of the transformational experience is the solution. Like the outworn cocoon shed by the caterpillar that has turned into a butterfly, racial prejudice will be shed. What will emerge from the cocoon is a human being with a fresh outlook, a true understanding of the natural structure of humanity, and an awareness that what they believe now has always been true. The new aware-ness generates within the awakened participant a desire to function as a tireless force for unity within the community. Operating out of a genuine belief in the oneness of humankind, people will have a more compassion-ate attitude toward one another than most men and women do today. While they will no longer tolerate any manifestation of prejudice, they will be compassionate toward those who are still caught in the mesh of white supe-riority, steadfastly believing that all human beings can experience a change of heart. Thus there will be no need to lobby for legislation eradicating those overt and subtle institutional practices that have fostered racism. Having internalized the truth about the oneness of the human family, there will be no debating whether such legislation should be passed. Composed of socially enlightened men and women, the institutions themselves will willingly identify and root out those practices. There will be no equivocat-ing over whether it is the right thing to do. The desire to right the pro-longed, grievous wrong of racism will spring from the core of their souls.

Without transformation it is impossible to attain such a social state, and the only seemingly rational recourse is to employ programs to "manage" racism. We know this to be a desperate exercise in hopelessness. Genuine involvement in the transformational experience of the Institutes for the Healing of Racism turns skeptics into believers that humans can change their outlook, attitudes, and behavior.

We have found that the major stumbling block to healing racism through transformation is the prevalence of the belief that human beings cannot be changed. Sadly, many leading academics share this flawed notion, which has influenced the thinking of most lay people. This view has been influ-enced by outdated, warped theories of past philosophers, scientists, and theologians (for further information on this subject, see Nathan Rutstein's

Coming of Age at the Millennium: Embracing the Oneness of Humankind).
Modern science recognizes that everything in nature—which obviously includes humans—is subject to change. In fact, the only thing that doesn't change is change itself.

For this reason the Institutes for the Healing of Racism place considerable emphasis on knowing the true nature of the human being, who is meant to be dynamic, endowed with great potential for goodness and wisdom. Influencing the Institutes' thinking on this subject is paleontologist and theologian Pierre Teilhard de Chardin's view of the reality of man: "We are not human beings having a spiritual experience; we are spiritual beings having a human experience." In other words, we are a soul with a body and not a body with a soul. The distinction is great. In reality, the soul has a body that is subject to the laws of composition and decomposition. The soul, however, is everlasting. Think of the soul as a light focused on a mirror, which is the body. The light, or soul, is not attached to the mirror, or body; nor is the light inside of the mirror, yet there is a mysterious association between the two. Should the mirror break, the light continues to shine nonetheless.

The soul is endowed with the potential for growth, or continual positive change. As the soul—which is our reality and the animating force of all human beings—develops, it becomes aware of realities that remain hidden to those who reject the notion of a soul or neglect its development. One of those realities is the oneness of humankind. Once that reality is discovered, there is no going back, and there is a natural urge to share with others what you have discovered.

Those who undergo the transformational experience of the Institutes for the Healing of Racism find themselves gaining insights into the nature of humanity through soul-to-soul communication. The experience itself, rather than any a lecture, convinces participants that the soul is their reality, not the body.

A GROWING AWARENESS

For most participants transformation does not occur instantaneously during the Institutes for the Healing of Racism experience. Usually, the transformation comes about as the result of a shift in consciousness that takes place over an extended period of time. However, there have been a few cases in which genuine transformation took place after only two sessions.

Those who are committed to the process will notice that they are more focused on the "real" as opposed to the superficial. They will place greater credence on a person's values, his or her spiritual qualities such as trustworthiness, compassion, love, truthfulness, and courtesy, rather than on his or her skin color, clothes, and social or economic status. They will develop a penetrative sight capable of distinguishing between fact and fiction, capable of sensing the reality of others. They become more aware of the true essence of a human being. Consequently they discover and develop potentialities within themselves that they never knew they possessed.

Participants also become more "heart-centered" than "head-centered." In other words, they find themselves becoming more sensitive to others' feelings. They rely more and more on their intuition to discern the truth, and in their interactions with others. This doesn't mean they have chosen to abandon use of their cognitive powers. All it means is that they have adopted a more balanced approach to assessing situations and maintaining relationships. They know that relying primarily on brainpower in their human interactions often leads to superficial understanding.

Those involved in the process of healing racism usually discover their spiritual potentialities, which enables them to discover that thinking analytically isn't the only way to think. By realizing that we are essentially spiritual beings who are connected to our Creator, we can draw upon that Source for knowledge and wisdom. This is called transcendent thinking. Unlike analytical thinking, which often produces tension, transcendent thinking is a peaceful experience. Moreover, it is a joyful experience, for it produces inspirational thoughts without warning and without effort. It is a practice that is so simple that most university-trained individuals are unaware of it or reject it without even trying it, brushing it aside as too simplistic.

We do not advocate abandoning analytical thinking, for clearly there is a place for it. It is necessary for doing one's taxes and other chores requiring calculation and analysis. It is not, however, the mode that produces fresh ideas, for it relies on one's memory bank and life experiences as a database. To find answers to abstract questions or new problems, or to create something new, an analytical thinker processes acquired knowledge. What is produced may be logical, but it is not new. It is usually a rehash of what was done in the past with a new name and a new look. Experience is not always the best teacher.

When one thinks analytically, the mind is in a computer-like mode; whereas the transcendent thinker is in a receptive mode. In such a receptive state, the thinker empties his consciousness of all thoughts and memories and awaits insights. The insights come, but we need to trust that they will come. Doubts are thoughts, which block the flow of insights. Having our minds and hearts cluttered with acquired knowledge while attempting to be receptive shuts the door to the divine flow. Frustration results, and our skepticism is reinforced, in turn deflating our will to be receptive. When we slip into such a mindset, we unwittingly cut ourselves off from the most reliable Source of guidance in this life.

How do we know that transcendent thinking works? We have experienced it. We have learned that setting aside our acquired knowledge and memories enables us to become a clear channel for God's guidance. It has dawned on us that this act is an expression of faith, a sincere prayer—that God is aware of our concerns, problems, and interests, and that they will be addressed at the appropriate time in the form of meaningful insights. This, to the beholder, is a confirmation that transcendent thinking works. The more we rely on transcendent thinking, the more it becomes a natural reflex.

Since prejudice is an unquestioned emotional attachment to a falsehood assumed to be the truth, participants in the Institutes for the Healing of Racism eventually let go of that stifling commitment. They become more curious, more open to new ideas, more accepting and respectful of others regardless of skin color, culture, religion, or ethnicity. Their first instinct is to see the good in others. They are no longer captives of a rigid set of principles based on distortions of the truth. They become more adventurous, more willing to explore new avenues of social thought. They are exposed to the full scope of wonderment. As a result they gain a new enthusiasm for life.

With these new insights, participants develop a deep appreciation of the transformational process. They grow more patient and persevering and less impulsive. They realize that healing the disease of racism is impossible without transformation; thus they become more process-oriented than event-oriented. If they continue to be involved in the healing process, they look forward to each new day as an opportunity to learn something new about themselves and their community. Life becomes an exciting adventure, and the ideal of a united humanity becomes more and more possible. In time, they see that it is not only possible, it is meant to be.

Tyrone R. Baines, an official at the Kellogg Foundation, agrees. He agrees because his racial healing experience enabled him to have a change of heart about his view of race relations in America. Until recently, he felt he could never get rid of his anger:

I grew up as a migrant farm worker in the 1960s in rural Virginia, Maryland, and Delaware. I remember the farm owner saying it was too hot to dig the potatoes; so let's wait until the sun goes down and start digging again.

The farm owner's message was clear. What he was saying was that it was too hot for the potatoes and not too hot for me. He was more concerned about damaging the potatoes than damaging me and my folks. I had a series of incidents like this in my life, which made me very angry, and I joined the Black power movement. Eldridge Cleaver and Malcolm X were my heroes.

I carried this anger for many years, and then the Institute for the Healing of Racism came along. I went to a two-day workshop, really prepared to let the white author of the book *Healing Racism in America* know how little he knew about racism. After all, I read all of the books on racism, taught black studies and lived with it. At the end of the first day, I admitted that I had the disease and wanted to be healed. I began my healing process, and I am still healing, but now I wake up in the morning without that anger, a burden I have carried for so many years.

AN EDUCATIONAL EXPERIENCE

An educational component is built into the transformational program of the Institutes for the Healing of Racism. Participants learn about their true racial conditioning, become aware of how it developed, and learn how to change it. They also become aware of the nature of racism, its origins in their country, and its impact on the nation as a whole.

The educational process is directed at both the mind and heart, for both need to be educated. Educating the mind alone won't get to the core of the problem, because those who are in denial will remain there. Educating the heart produces the will to change one's racial conditioning. Our universities are packed with people who know a great deal about racism but lack the courage to explore their hearts to see how they have been affected by the social malady they oppose intellectually. Consequently they have had little or no success in overcoming racism. When their efforts falter, they eventually become champions of the enterprise to "manage" racism.

At the same time, educating only the heart produces people who feel liberated from the poisonous clutches of racism but are unequipped to explain to others what makes them feel free. In some cases it can lead to fanaticism, the manufacturing of "facts" to support one's position, exaggeration, or melodramatic behavior that offends sincere seekers of racial healing.

Balance is required. At each two-hour Institute session, participants gain knowledge and then engage in the dialogue of the spirit, which is designed to educate the heart. The first thirty minutes is devoted to educating the mind by sharing information on some aspect of one of three themes: the oneness of humankind, the origins of racism, or the pathology of racism and how it affects us. More time is devoted to educating the heart because it takes longer to purge oneself of comfortable, lifelong beliefs and feelings than it does to acquire knowledge.

While it is recommended that the information presented during the first thirty minutes of each session be an Institute participant, it is acceptable for a knowledgeable individual who is not a participant to give a presentation. It is preferable for participants to do the presentations because they usually learn a great deal from preparing for the presentation and because it gives them experience and helps to develop effective communication skills.

The presentations vary in format. They can be given in the form of a lecture, a discussion, a slide show, or video. They can be a combination of methods. For example, a young woman in New London, Connecticut, once organized a presentation on an aspect of the oneness of humankind. She had someone read a short essay by anthropologist Ashley Montague, then showed an original fifteen-minute slide show emphasizing scientific proofs of the oneness of the human family. She concluded with the reading of three poems written by famous poets on the theme of oneness. Copies of the essay, the slide-show script, and the poems were handed out to all of the participants.

Every presenter is obligated to distribute handouts of the material covered in the presentation, and participants should keep them in a notebook. Usually, by the end of the ten-week program everyone has a fairly thick notebook.

We have discovered that the process of preparing and sharing information sets off in the participants a hunger for more knowledge. People who have had no formal training in research become avid pursuers of information pertaining to the three themes covered in the presentations. They find themselves spending more time in the library than ever before, and some become passionate explorers of the Internet. If they come across something interesting in the local newspaper, they make note of it with the idea of sharing it with their fellow participants. Even when they are not preparing for a presentation they will often come to a session with photocopied materials and hand them out to everyone. There are times when ten or more participants will come to a meeting with handouts.

It is wonderful to see this enthusiasm for knowledge displayed, especially among those who never went to college or never finished high school. Witnessing this kind of behavior assures us that an important aim of the Institutes is being achieved. The Institutes for the Healing of Racism aim to help every participant become able to articulate with knowledge, wisdom, conviction, and power the scientific and spiritual proofs of the oneness of humankind; explain how racism originated in their country; and describe the pathology of racism and how it affects us.

By achieving this aim, the Institutes have created a cadre of enlightened men and women who are able to recruit others into a growing grassroots campaign of racial transformation. It is heartening to see that amassing such knowledge doesn't turn the participants into racial know-it-alls or gurus. There are no experts in the Institutes for the Healing of Racism. We gladly share in the spirit of service what we have learned. The fact that there is no end to the learning process helps participants develop and maintain a humble attitude. Also, knowing one's own place in the healing process keeps the participant humble. A further safeguard against developing an arrogant or superior attitude is knowing that one is essentially a healer who is familiar with the interior suffering of those in need of healing. The racial healer is able to feel compassion and empathy much more easily and quickly than they could before their involvement in the Institutes for the Healing of Racism.

FOSTERING THE ONENESS
OF HUMANKIND

Why do the Institutes for the Healing of Racism place such great emphasis on the oneness of humankind?

There are a number of reasons. First, it is a fundamental truth, and unfortunately, the great majority of people on our planet are unaware of it. They have a fractured view of the structure of humanity and sense that the racial and ethnic divisions existing between people are part of nature's grand design.

We have discovered that when first approached with the idea of the reality of oneness, most people resist changing their view. Many brush off the approach as too simplistic or Pollyannish. But if they persist in attending sessions of the Institutes for the Healing of Racism, their resistance breaks down; they find themselves no longer emotionally attached to the falsehood they once assumed to be the truth. In fact, they become enthusiastic promulgators of the principle of the oneness of humankind.

A case in point exists in Vermilion, South Dakota. Ten White teenagers who felt people of color were inherently inferior to them destroyed an

American Indian holy place. The county judge found them guilty of a hate crime and ordered them to attend a ten-week program of the Institutes for the Healing of Racism.

When the ten young people completed the program, they had a different attitude toward people of color. They had embraced the principle of the oneness of humankind and saw American Indians as their brothers and sisters. They apologized to the Indian leadership for desecrating their holy place and volunteered to help rebuild it. Moreover, they began teaching their parents, relatives, and friends about the oneness of humankind.

A second reason for emphasizing the oneness of humankind is that universal internalization of this reality will lead to the end of racism. People will no longer be influenced by racial stereotypes; they will no longer believe that there are inherently superior and inferior groups of people; and they will no longer believe that there are distinct races. They will, instead, embrace wholeheartedly the reality that there is only one race—the human race. They will be able to articulate with knowledge, wisdom, and conviction the following observation by anthropologist Ashley Montague: "The idea of race is man's most dangerous myth."

Some of the world's leading experts in genetics, anthropology, biology, paleontology, and social psychology gathered in Austria in the summer of 1995 to assess the scientific validity of the concept of race. Summarizing their scholarly discussions, anthropologist Lionel Tiger has written,

The fact is that all contemporary population genetics and molecular biology underscores that the nineteenth century notion of races as discrete and different entities is false. There is only gradual genetic diversity between groups. We all emerge smoothly into each other. Nearly all of the physically observable differences reflect very limited local adaptations to climate and other specific environmental conditions. ("Tiger, Lionel, Trump Race Card," *Wall Street Journal,* 23, Feb., 1996)*

As they learn and eventually accept the principle of the oneness of humankind through the Institutes' transformation process, participants do not revert to their old racial views. Instead, they become advocates of a positive, unific belief. Wholehearted engagement in the transformational experience guarantees that result. However, this does not happen to those who only purge themselves of an old belief without replacing it with belief in the oneness of humanity. In time, the vacuum is filled by the old belief. The same thing can happen to individuals who fail to completely rid themselves of the old belief in racial superiority and simply adopt a new belief in addition to it. In most cases the old belief is dominant. Because it is more familiar, the individual is emotionally attached to it and therefore trusts it more than the new one. When this happens, the newly adopted belief becomes a cover-up for the old. Most people in racial denial are plagued with this condition.

It is important to stress the principle of the oneness of humankind because its omission in race-relations efforts has proven counterproductive. Emphasizing only diversity can lead to the creation of a sophisticated form of apartheid within a community in which African Americans and Whites, Arabs and Jews, Hispanics and Asians rarely interact. This is evident on college campuses and in school cafeterias. After work most people retreat to their ethnically friendly neighborhoods, where their distorted views of other

---

* For more proofs of the oneness of humankind, see Nathan Rutstein, *Coming of Age at the Millennium: Embracing the Oneness of Humankind.*

ethnic groups is continually reinforced. If they do meet with other groups at all, it is usually at an annual race unity picnic or a multicultural arts festival at which people exchange artifacts. Emphasis on the differences between groups of people and a lack of regular, meaningful interaction between the groups reinforces the urge to stay with one's own kind. Giving in to the urge, which is fueled by fear and ignorance, creates a spawning ground for prejudice.

This emphasis on the principle of the oneness of humankind does not mean that the Institutes for the Healing of Racism reject cultural differences. In fact, the Institutes celebrate diversity while acknowledging the reality that everyone is related to one another. Recognizing that the physical and behavioral differences between peoples actually stems from oneness helps participants to gain a more complete picture of the composition of the human family.

While all things are interrelated, every living thing is different. This paradoxical aspect of reality manifests itself in the principle of unity in diversity. In nature, no two things are exactly alike, yet they all stem from the same reality. Every cell in our body is unique, as is each snowflake, each rose of the same color. Within a litter of puppies, each puppy has its own temperament, coloring, and size. No two human beings, including identical twins, have an identical set of fingerprints. None of a tree's branches, twigs, leaves, blossoms, or fruits are exactly alike, yet they are all a part of the whole, tied to one set of roots, which are tied to the soil, as well as the Sun and the rain, the source of their nutrients.

An excellent illustration of the principle of unity in diversity can be seen in the structure of the human body. Though the heart, lungs, pancreas, liver, stomach, and kidneys all have different functions, they must operate harmoniously if the body is to manifest good health. They are some of the essential parts that make up the whole. In and of itself, none of these parts has any real value, but together they have a purpose.

There are reasons why the popular trend in the race relations field is to stress differences and ignore oneness. There are those who are simply ignorant of the reality of the oneness of the human family and the interrelatedness of all things. They sincerely believe that ensuring respect for all cultures will achieve racial harmony. When the longed-for harmony doesn't materialize, they either give up the cause or try to convince themselves and others that they are making headway.

There are groups who do not promote the principle of the oneness of humankind, even some who, could benefit from it in the long run. Some elements among the traditional targets of racism, like the Pan-Africanists and members of the Black Power movement avoid focusing on oneness because they feel it would diminish their effort to develop pride in their newly found culture. The pride, they feel, helps African Americans, Hispanics, Asians, and American Indians overcome feelings of inferiority and self-hatred and gain greater confidence and self-esteem. Some who are involved in the cultural pride effort fear that the call for oneness is a call for uniformity based on the notion that everyone should adopt the "White man's" way of life. While this attitude helps to reinforce the prevailing fractured view of the structure of humanity, it is understandable why an oppressed people who have been cut off from their rich cultural heritage would want to become familiar with it and with their ancestral roots. It is a right that should not be denied. However, there are those men and women who use the cultural pride enrichment endeavor to bolster their campaign for power. To achieve their end, they intensify the suspicion, anger, bitterness, and resentment toward their real or imagined oppressors. Those who follow these demagogues develop a pride rooted in hatred and a distorted sense of superiority that usually evolves into a virulent prejudice.

Some supporters of the multicultural movement use it to promote a hidden desire to block the community's acceptance of the oneness of humankind. They purposely stress cultural differences in their slick programs and presentations to preserve the "purity" of their own culture and prevent its extinction. Hundreds of institutions that purchase these programs are so desperate to find ways to avoid racial eruptions in schools or places of work that they are unable to detect the real purpose of the programs. As a result, their fear is easily exploited to spread the wrong message.

The advocates of cultural purity, operating within the purview of multiculturalism, seem to be achieving their goal of institutionalizing cultural separatism. This is cleverly done by billboarding terms such as "tolerance" and "respect" in their literature and public pronouncements, terms we associate with goodness, human rights, justice, and equality. They are terms most people of good will are attracted to and feel comfortable with. Taking advantage of the prevailing fears associated with interracial encounters and the desire for social tranquility, the sophisticated purveyors of cultural separatism have defined tolerance and respect as a condition in which every culture is allowed to do its own thing without any positive or negative interference from outsiders. To uphold the image of human rights advocates, they may engage in charity work for the economically disadvantaged of other ethnic groups, and they may participate in an intercultural festival once or twice a year, but regular intercultural fraternizing is frowned upon.

It isn't surprising that the multiculural programs whose real intent is to preserve cultural separatism never urge people of different ethnic groups to love one another. The word "love" is missing from their texts because love can lead to unity, which involves the serious mixing and banding together of ethnic groups. As a result, one rarely sees the word "unity" in their materials either. What is vigorously emphasized instead—often through dazzling presentations—is an appreciation of one another's differences. Perhaps the greatest evidence of their success is that love and unity are not mentioned as goals in present-day race relations conferences, speeches, and literature. The leading race relations pundits avoid those terms. We think it was Dr. Martin Luther King, Jr., who was the last American human rights light to proclaim passionately in public the need for all people to learn to love one another so that true unity could be realized in America.

FACILITATION

Facilitating a dialogue of the spirit is unlike facilitating a conventional group dialogue. Possessing a cultivated intuition, compassion, empathy, and humility are required, as is the ability to keep participants focused and abiding by the dialoguing guidelines.

Effective facilitators view themselves as servants of the group, committed to helping each participant gain something meaningful from the healing process. They try hard not to judge, evaluate, or analyze the participants, trying instead to take to heart everyone's shared thoughts and feelings. Everyone's expression is appreciated, even the explosive expressions. In fact, effective facilitators consider a participant's unleashing of rage as a compliment, for the outburst is interpreted as a sign that participant feels safe enough to share their true feelings. When a participant explodes, the facilitators assure the troubled individual that it is okay to explode, and they provide as much support as possible. Such a response not only subdues other participants' fears, it also models a way to handle potentially difficult situations. A seemingly negative act is turned into a positive experience for all.

Unlike conventional facilitators, Institutes' facilitators are not aloof referees. They are full-fledged participants who are ready and willing to share their feelings. They do not view themselves as experts, but rather as experienced participants who need more healing. One of the worst things facilitators can do is to give the impression that they are completely healed. Such nonverbal messages create a superior-inferior atmosphere within the group and inhibit honest sharing. Effective facilitators try to convey the idea that we all come together on an equal basis in need of healing. We have learned that this approach puts participants at ease and promotes the willingness to be forthcoming. Knowing that those who are leading the discussion share in the struggles that are common to all has a bonding effect on both participants and facilitators.

There have been cases when professional psychologists have failed as facilitators. They have failed because they communicated nonverbally an air of superiority, giving the impression that they were immune to the disease of racism. This kind of attitude leaves participants feeling that they have been judged, evaluated, analyzed, and found to be inferior. As a result, they resist sharing openly and instead share only what will impress the highly credentialed facilitator, saying what they believe the facilitator wants to hear.

To be an effective facilitator requires more than a great deal of compassion and humility. It requires personal experience with the dialogue of the spirit—and not just once, but many times. This is essential because it affords an appreciation for the kind of atmosphere that results in healthy sharing and listening. The more facilitators experience the dialogue of the spirit, the more capable they become of sensing the reality of others. They know there are no wrong comments in sharing, for individuals who are sharing become aware of their true racial conditioning and learn their true feelings about race. The facilitators understand that this is important because it enables the sharers to know what they have to work on. It means a healthy start has been made.

The facilitators' responses must be encouraging and should inspire sharers to continue the healing process. When sharers are having difficulty articulating their thoughts and feelings, the facilitators should be able to ask questions or make comments that help the participants release a gnawing buried feeling or see an aspect of reality that has previously eluded them. Having gone through the dialogue of the spirit many times, the facilitators will have memorized and internalized the guidelines and can therefore ensure that everyone abides by them. This is crucial, because a lackadaisical attitude toward monitoring the guidelines can lead to ego clashes, unsolicited advice, cross talk, arguments, and a complete shutdown of the dialogue of the spirit.

Effective facilitators have undergone "reconditioning," replacing conventional facilitating practices with the dialogue of the spirit facilitation practices. Such facilitators have shed one set of habits for another. This transformation helps them to become more caring human beings, possessing an acute ability to sense others' true feelings.

Ideally, every session should have two facilitators, sitting side by side, who share the work equally. They should be of different skin color or gender. This pairing is more than symbolic of the oneness of humankind, for it demonstrates a genuine appreciation and respect for one another. This dashes the myth that people of different ethnic origin can't get along very well or can't be united in thought and purpose. Kidding one another goes a long way toward underscoring the mutual respect and appreciation the facilitators feel for each other. It also helps to lighten the atmosphere and put participants at ease.

There is a very practical reason for having two facilitators: Listening with the heart to every participant's sharing can be emotionally draining. It is good to have some relief. If one facilitator is emotionally overcome, the other can stand in for a while.

Effective facilitators try to avoid harsh or sarcastic comments. Not that they are wishy-washy or Pollyannish. When it comes to defending a principle or upholding a dialoguing guideline, facilitators must be firm but compassionate.

Unlike conventional facilitators of dialogue, effective Institutes' facilitators don't try to conceal their true emotions. If they are moved to cry, they cry. That encourages participants to let go of self-imposed emotional restraints. Usually when this happens, whatever obstacles to communication existed between group members vanishes, and participants feel a natural urge to reach each other and bond.

There is a special procedure for going over the guidelines before the group dialogue begins. To replace old and familiar interpersonal communications practices with new practices, it is helpful to repeat why the guidelines are always read aloud, always emphasizing the benefits of adhering to the guidelines. Changing attitudes and behavior is not easy! After seeing again and again the positive effects that come from adhering to the guidelines, facilitators naturally find themselves internalizing the guidelines.

A sheet containing fifteen written guidelines is passed around. Each person reads one guideline. To ensure that what has been read has had time to register, the person who reads the guideline waits three or four seconds before passing the sheet to the next person. After the last guideline is read, the facilitators reveal two other guidelines: (1) Never engage in a one-on-one discussion with the person next to you while someone is sharing. It is not only discourteous; it may give the impression that something negative is being said about the person who is sharing. (2) The other unwritten guideline is never to approach a participant after the dialogue session with unsolicited advice. Whatever is shared in the group is confidential, and there is the risk that the person who has shared may view the advice as a patronizing expression of superiority.

In summary, effective facilitators are people who listen with the heart, who genuinely want to help participants join in the healing process. They see their work not as a performance but as a service. To possess such an attitude, they embrace wholeheartedly the philosophy and psychology of the Institutes for the Healing of Racism and believe that it will overcome the skepticism of some participants.

In the beginning psychologist John Barrett of Marshall, Michigan, was a skeptical participant. He explains,

I feel blessed by an extraordinary, two day experience that I shared with forty others. Its memory is strong and its legacy permeates my daily existence. It was a gift from God through the efforts of two special human beings who could purely express the deeper reality of humanity, our spiritual oneness with each other.

How did they do this? It was not clever or sophisticated, well practiced or highly trained. It was pure, it was experiential, it was clarity, it was the power of love. What does this look like? What is its feel, its rhythm, its texture?

Their presence was authentic, not packaged. When their eyes moved across the audience, it was not mechanical or cold like a lighthouse. It was not restless or needy, seeking agreement or appreciation. It was not still, self-absorbed and searching for the next line or right phrase. Their attention was tender and lingering, warm and intimate, receptive and inviting, affectionate and moving. It was calm and moved naturally, never measured or planned.

Their presence was authentic, not practiced. The first time they said we were their brothers and sisters, my eyes widened; the second time, I frowned; the third time, I smirked; the fourth time, I took a deep breath; the fifth time, I smiled; the sixth time I accepted; the seventh time, I embraced.

Their presence was authentic, not professional. When someone else was troubled, caught between emotions, the two stopped, looked within and then from a deep sense of rightness they moved to that person's side to embrace them. They moved with a calm and deep stillness that seemed anchored and sure. Their arms enfolded the tearful person in an embrace that somehow was total and yet sensitive to the integrity of the individual.

Their presence was authentic, not polished. When someone shared an insight that shone a light into their own hearts and exposed the fragile, ugly, limited and scared; they treasured the beauty of the moment, of the person, of the communal sharing. Sometimes, in their profound appreciation, tears ran freely down their faces.

Their presence was authentic, not performance. The experience was not bound by their egos and its natural needs. There was spiritual transaction, beyond words and even beyond actions. The truth was channeled through their presence and resonated within us, creating a sweet harmony of shared understanding that still echoes today.

Their presence was authentic, not perfection. They greeted you so generously with smiles, easy affection, hugs without reservation, and warm contacts of spontaneous love.

Does it sound magical, somewhat unreal? No, it was spiritual and so abundantly real that it awakened a deep thirst for the oneness of humanity and the healing of racism.

THE TWO-DAY WORKSHOP

The two-day workshop is an essential part of the Institutes for the Healing of Racism experience. For most participants it is their first experience, the beginning of their racial healing. The aim of the workshop is to motivate participants to continue the healing process. It is designed to generate hope and optimism that the disease of racism can be healed. At its end, most participants find themselves at the threshold of hope, peering at the pathway to healing and wanting to make the journey.

The workshop offers a preview of what participants will experience in the ten-session cycle. They become aquatinted with the session format as well as with the philosophy and psychology of the Institutes for the Healing of Racism.

The number of participants at a workshop should be no more than thirty-five and no less than four. It is important that there be a strong representation of diverse ethnic groups. Part of the healing therapy involves sensing the true feelings of other participants who have been infected or wounded by racism. When that happens over an extended period of time, compassion replaces suspicion, contentment replaces insecurity, knowledge replaces ignorance, anger dissipates, and bonding occurs between people who once distrusted one another. Many people who have participated in the workshop go away believing that such transformation can take place. They are no longer captives of skepticism.

The two workshop facilitators should come from different ethnic backgrounds. Neither one should dominate. When one gives a presentation, the other facilitates the dialogue of the spirit, and vice versa.

The workshop opens with one of the facilitators warmly welcoming everyone and asking them to give their name and share what they hope to get out of the workshop. Participants are also asked to reveal any apprehensions they may be harboring.

The other facilitator follows by describing the kinds of feelings most participants experience during the two-day healing session. Participants are warned that the first day may be so emotionally draining, so psychologically challenging that they may be seized by an urge to not attend the second day. The facilitator explains what will set off these feelings, pointing out that the workshop format is designed to challenge in a non-confrontational manner the participants' racial mindset, with which they have been comfortable for many years. After all, it has helped them in the past to avoid pain or embarrassment during other interracial encounters. Survival is usually the driving force in the formation of one's racial mindset. A lot of energy and time has been expended in forging the mindset, which is usually a mixture of fear, suspicion, misinformation, half-truths, distorted perceptions, biases, and an aversion to physical and mental pain.

The facilitator further explains that there is a natural desire to cling to the mindset. When it is challenged, a painful conflict is usually set off in the participants. It is a case of the familiar old resisting the unfamiliar new. Fear sets off the resistance to dismantling the mindset, and participants are seized by the impulse to stay away the second day. However, when participants are told that the conflict is actually a sign of progress because it means the dismantling of their racial mindset—the first step in the transformational process—has begun, the participants are more willing to come back the next day.

The facilitator goes on to explain that the second day usually turns out to be a festival of joy. Participants sense the possibilities of changing their racial attitudes and behavior. Because they have been exposed to the dialogue of the spirit, they see the potential of bonding with people whom they would have avoided in the past. For the first time, Whites become aware that their racial mindset is a barrier to freedom from racial prejudice, and people of color sense themselves breaking out of the cage of internalized racism. All begin to appreciate the need to challenge their racial mindset.

The same facilitator describes the distinguishing features of the Institutes for the Healing of Racism. The following list provides a fairly comprehensive description of the distinguishing features:

1. The Institutes for the Healing of Racism view racism as a disease.

2. The Institutes for the Healing of Racism engage participants in a transformational experience.

3. The Institutes for the Healing of Racism emphasize love and unity instead of tolerance.

4. The Institutes for the Healing of Racism view internalization of the principle of the oneness of humankind as a vaccine against the disease of racism.

5. The Institutes for the Healing of Racism are an ongoing healing process.

6. While the Institutes do not promote any particular religious creed, they are spiritually centered.

Next a facilitator describes the shifts in consciousness that occur in a participant who has gone through the ten-week cycle. Participants learn that they are likely to become more spiritually centered than materially oriented, more affective than cognitive in their relations with people, more curious than certain, and more transformation-centered than solution-driven.

A ten-minute break follows.

During the last phase of the workshop on the morning of the first day, participants watch two segments of a video showing a racially diverse group of men talking about racial issues in a heartfelt manner. An African-American man unleashes his fury at a well-meaning White liberal man's patronizing attitude of superiority. This segment illustrates the anger that many people of color live with and try to control. The enraged man reveals the many obstacles he has to overcome every day of his life because of the color of his skin and the texture of his hair. The White man, unaware of his patronizing and superior attitude, is taken aback. He feels as if he's being abused and misunderstood.

At this point the video is stopped, and the facilitator of color points out that he identifies with the young man who released the fury of his rage at the White man. He cites some experiences in his own past and present that have fueled his lifelong anger. After his story is shared, the other facilitator introduces the next segment of the video, which demonstrates that, despite the African-American man's angry outburst and the White man's patronizing attitude of superiority, the two men are able to overcome their differences and bond.

In the second segment of the video, the moderator of the dialogue asks the White fellow two simple but penetrating questions that help him to sense the African-American man's pain and anguish. When the African-

American man senses that the White man, whom he has known for a number of years, finally understands why he's angry, he says in a calm voice, "Now I can work with you."

When the White man responds, saying, "I want to help you, but I don't know how," the African-American man's reaction is, "The best way to help me is for you to help yourself become race-prejudice free."

At that point the video is shut off, and the White facilitator explains that he identifies with the White man in the video. He shares with participants some of the experiences he has had in identifying his infection of racism and what he has tried to do to heal it.

After lunch one of the facilitators describes the different stages of the dialogue of the spirit and shares with the participants the dialoguing guidelines. Then the other facilitator launches the group into a three-phased dialogue on the question, "When you see or hear the word 'racism,' what images come to mind, and what emotions are generated within you?"

While describing the two goals and the five steps to achieving them (see Part 2, "Goals and Aims"), one facilitator describes the education of the mind and heart that occurs during each session of the Institutes for the Healing of Racism. The benefits derived from engaging in the educational process are explained.

After a ten-minute break, a presentation is made on the scientific proofs of the oneness of humankind, providing an example of the education of the mind. Afterward, the other facilitator starts the education of the heart phase by asking participants to meditate on the question, "When you see or hear the term 'oneness of humankind,' what images come to mind, and what emotions are generated within you, both positive and negative?" The same question is addressed in one-on-one sharing, then in group sharing. Of course, before group sharing begins, the facilitator has the group go over the guidelines and explains why they are read aloud before every group sharing, emphasizing that they help participants become proficient in listening with the heart.

For the last exercise of the first day, the participants are asked to rise, form a circle, and hold hands. A facilitator explains the nature of the human being, building the explanation on Pierre Teilhard de Chardin's statement, "We are not human beings having a spiritual experience; we are spiritual beings having a human experience." The sharing of spiritual proofs of the oneness of humankind follows.

At the beginning of the second day, both facilitators have something positive to say in greeting the participants. The first exercise includes a presentation about how racism developed in our country. It is essentially a historical overview of how the disease of racism began and evolved. Afterward, the following question is posed to the group: "When you see or hear the terms 'holocaust,' 'slavery,' and 'Indian massacre,' what images come to mind, and what emotions are generated within you?" The other facilitator then gets the participants started with the three-phased dialogue of the spirit. During the group sharing, the facilitator who is not facilitating shares the Institutes' view that students of color are the object of genocide in our nation's schools.

After a ten-minute break an exercise that emphasizes the impact racism has had on Americans is started. Statistics are shared along with stories of some people who have been hurt or psychologically damaged by racism. The Arthur Ashe story is shared. Then the following question is posed to the group: "When you hear the Arthur Ashe story, in particular his observation that 'being an African-American in America is far more difficult to endure than having AIDS,' what images come to mind, and what emotions are generated within you?" In the group sharing that follows, the facilitator of color shares his view of the advantages of being White in our society.

After lunch, the workshop closes with an appreciation exercise. A facilitator explains why this is being done—that too often in our hurly-burly society little or no gratitude is expressed to others. The facilitator also points out that everyone has to participate in the exercise. One at a time, participants express their appreciation not only for family members, friends, and colleagues, but particularly for those in the room who have moved or enlightened them. The facilitators usually express their appreciation for one another.

When the appreciation exercise is completed, most of the participants are reluctant to leave. It seems as if they want to bask in the spirit of love that has been generated by the gratitude pouring forth from twenty-five or more open hearts. For many it is an unforgettable experience that leaves a lasting impression.

Reverend Jim Brazell of the First Presbyterian Church in Albion, Michigan, was so moved by such an experience that he shared his awakening in a local newspaper column:

I am a person of privilege that I did nothing to earn. I can walk into any store in town, pick up an item, and hold it as long as necessary to make up my mind. Few would suspect me of preparation to steal.

Salespersons do not add extra dollars to the purchase price when I enter a shop. I do not have to take medication for asthma, diabetes, or high blood pressure, or heart disease. No studies predict premature death in my future.

I can walk down the sidewalk, in a bad mood with a fierce look, in freedom. No woman would grasp her pocket book more tightly, no mother would clutch her child's hand more tightly as I approached them.

No decision about my shopping, my recreation, or my health is affected by the color of my skin. Because I am white.

Not quite true, every decision about my shopping, my recreation, or my health is affected by my skin color. The results are always in my favor. Remember, I am a person of privilege.

The Healing Racism seminar last weekend brought this to mind and heart. As a man of moderate convictions, I have always found prejudice easy to deplore. It has been someone else's problem. As a minister, I have found it easy to talk the talk without walking the walk on racially informed topics.

This time I could not run away from my prejudices. The assumptions that always made things go my way were very carefully challenged. Thirty-one persons shared their stories, their pain, their struggles for self-respect and dignity. They told their story in a culture that listens first to the white side, and then to the others, if there is time, if at all.

Stories told in a group are like pieces of a jig-saw puzzle. Once the first piece is placed on the board, then the other pieces find themselves by fitting its curved, sharp, and flat edges.

We were able to fit ourselves into a picture puzzle of Albion residents and workers who are more willing to speak out against racially oppressive actions and words and structures.

We will not permit the disease of racism which infects white people and wounds persons of color to continue to plague us, our neighbors, our family, our friends and our community.

I ask you to join the healing, for your own good, and for mine.

FROM INSTITUTE
TO INSTITUTION

Every organization needs to be administered, and the Institutes for the Healing of Racism are no exception.

In the beginning little thought was given to managing the Institutes. All we thought about was healing. But as what we were doing grew more popular, it became apparent that some management of our activities was necessary. There had to be some entity that set policy, promoted the program, dealt with the news media, administered the funds, published a newsletter, and handled inquiries, scheduling, and logistics.

Today every effective Institute for the Healing of Racism has a steering committee that is either elected by the general membership or is composed of committed volunteers. If there is an election, it is carried out in a way that reflects the philosophy of the Institutes: There are no candidates and no self-promotion. A secret ballot is used to determine who is most qualified to serve on the steering committee. Ideally, those persons who are most service-oriented, most selfless, who put cause ahead of personal gratification, are the most effective steering committee members. A deep understanding of the problem of racism is also helpful. An odd number of committee members should be elected. This prevents ties in decision-making votes. The number shouldn't exceed nine, because the larger the committee is, the more difficult it becomes to reach consensus and manage the affairs of the Institute.

Those Institutes that opt for the steering committee to be made up of volunteers should guard against admitting those who view serving on the steering committee as a position of political power or high status. Every Institute member, who is a potential steering committee member, should be aware of the Institutes' administrative as well as healing philosophy and procedure. It is important to note that the Institutes' view of power is different than the prevailing view, which is concerned with control, dominance, influence, and self-promotion. The Institutes see power as an opportunity to serve with humility. Those who serve the most are viewed as the most powerful.

Officers—that is, the secretary, treasurer, public information officer, chairperson, and vice-chairperson—are usually elected annually by the members of the steering committee. Again, the election is conducted by secret ballot, devoid of any form of campaigning. In time, Institute members learn to view self-promotion as an offensive act, and anyone involved in self-promotion doesn't end up on the steering committee.

The steering committee views itself as a vehicle for serving the Institute's membership and the community-at-large. While no member has any authority, the committee can empower a member to exert authority in dealing with a particular issue. When dealing with that issue, the chosen person will inform those with whom they must work that the committee has authorized them to speak for the committee.

Only the body, and not any single member of it, makes decisions. The decisions are made through consultation. By consultation we don't mean simple discussion or negotiation, nor is lobbying a factor. Consultation is essentially an exercise of service in which ego is set aside and the best interests of the Institute become the primary focus. For example, when a committee member offers an idea to the Institute, it is offered in the spirit of service, and every response to the offering is appreciated, be it negative or positive. If the committee members feel that the idea has little merit, the individual may provide more information to clarify the idea. But if the members reject it, the individual does not sulk but accepts the committee's decision as an act that will benefit the Institute. In other words, pushing one's idea at all costs is discouraged.

Oftentimes ideas that are offered will inspire other members to build on them, and it doesn't take long before they find themselves involved in an exciting collective building process. In the end, the result is a decision that is based on an idea may have a very different appearance than when it was first introduced.

To consult properly requires discipline. There are no cross talk, no preaching, no hidden agendas, no pushing of personal pet projects, nor giving advice. Listening with the heart is extremely helpful in effective consultation. The ideal steering committee is composed of men and women who truly value one another as human beings. When this is so, everyone's contribution is wholeheartedly considered.

The general membership is an essential arm of the administration of the Institute. The steering committee, which appreciates this arrangement, meets on a regular basis with the rest of the Institute members. It looks upon the membership as a source of fresh ideas and suggestions and genuinely solicits members' offerings. Oftentimes the germ of an important steering committee decision is generated at the membership-steering committee meetings. The same principles of consultation are applied to these dialogues as are applied during the deliberations of the steering committee.

All members are encouraged to submit in writing to the steering committee questions to be used for future dialogues of the spirit. Such offerings can be made anytime by letter, fax, or e-mail. The idea is to build up a reliable storehouse of questions. These questions should be offered to other Institutes to help reinforce the cooperative spirit between Institutes, and build up their storehouse of questions.

To give sharper focus to the Institute's vision, the steering committee drafts an annual plan. The membership has a hand in this endeavor. It is encouraged to submit ideas to the steering committee. When the rough draft of the plan is drawn up, it is shared with the membership for its review. The committee seriously considers each member's input and proceeds with drawing up the final draft, which is shared with the membership via mail and the Institute's newsletter.

Relatively new Institutes should avoid developing grandiose schemes. It is best to keep things simple in the beginning. The major thrust should be to keep the existing membership involved in personal healing and fellowship.

The following is a sample plan of a seasoned Institute for the Healing of Racism:

1. Those who have undergone a two-day workshop will be encouraged to continue their healing via the cluster to which they were assigned. The ten-session cluster will be made up of those participants who took part in the workshop. The cluster functions as a

mini-Institute, focusing primarily on the education of the mind and heart processes.

2. To recruit new members, fifteen two-day workshops will be held in different parts of town.

3. An Institute will be established in one elementary school (for teachers, administrators, and parents).

4. An Institute will be established in one church.

5. Start developing a race relations library, where local residents are encouraged to do research.

6. Establish a speakers bureau that will supply speakers to schools, churches, synagogues, fraternal organizations, governmental agencies, colleges, and corporations. The talks will be designed to motivate audiences to become involved in the racial healing process offered by the Institute.

7. Hold an annual Institute for the Healing of Racism retreat on a three-day holiday weekend. Besides providing an opportunity for lots of fellowship, this event will give the members an opportunity to assess the effectiveness of the Institute.

8. There will be four steering committee-membership meetings during the year.

9. The Institute will seek funding from three foundations, the local department of education, and the Inter-Faith Council.

10. Continued moral, educational, and financial support of the Institute's race unity workshop for youth. The workshop, which is made up of a diverse cross-section of high school youth, creates songs, dances, and raps that promote racial harmony. They perform at schools, education conferences, on television, and in cor-

porate diversity workshops. The workshop has a study component. Half of the time is devoted to understanding and internalizing the oneness of humankind; the other half to gaining an understanding of how racism originated in this country and of the pathology of racism and how it affects us. Through this exercise the youth gain considerable knowledge of genetics, biology, history, psychology, sociology, anthropology and economics. By engaging in the dialogue of the spirit, they learn to listen with the heart.

11. Continue the annual Institute for the Healing of Racism banquet, at which local citizens who have excelled in promoting racial harmony are honored.

To ensure that all of the plan's goals are achieved, the steering committee sets up eleven committees made up of men and women who are part of the Institute's general membership. Each committee is assigned one of the plan's goals.

Affairs depend upon means, of course. While the Institute is a not-for-profit organization, it needs funds to maintain itself. There are rental fees, photocopying and mailing expenses, electric bills, telephone bills, promotional expenses, transportation expenses, and refreshment costs. All Institutes are encouraged to apply for nonprofit status. This makes them eligible for foundation and governmental agency grants.

There are other ways of securing funds, for example, charging a fee for facilitating workshops and providing speakers to various public and private organizations. The fee can be based on a graduated scale: The wealthier the group, the higher the fee. There will be times when economically struggling groups will not be asked to pay anything.

Audio tapes and videotapes can be produced on subjects such as facilitating, the dialogue of the spirit, the oneness of humankind, the origins of racism, the pathology of the disease of racism, the philosophy and psychology of the Institutes for the Healing of Racism, and so forth. The tapes can be sold locally and nationally through various educational catalogs.

By purchasing books on race relations themes in bulk, the Institute can receive sizable discounts and then sell the books to workshop participants and others at the retail price, keeping the difference. Some Institutes operate bookstores in their libraries and actively promote books through the mass media.

It is important to note that whatever funds the local Institute is able to generate goes into keeping it alive and dynamic. It is not in the money-making business, nor does anyone receive a salary. However, those who function as facilitators are given honoraria when facilitating workshops that are funded by corporations or governmental agencies.

Administering an Institute for the Healing of Racism should be an act of love. With that kind of collective attitude, any sign of positive growth will give rise to a sense of joy among the members of the steering committee. This is much like the a sensation that a parent experiences when a child does well in school or shows kindness to a forlorn friend. The steering committee's joy will usually have an uplifting effect on the general membership.

THE TRANSFORMATION
OF A COMMUNITY

Embracing the Institutes for the Healing of Racism has changed the culture and broadened the outlook of one of America's leading human service institutions. Starr Commonwealth, which is headquartered in Albion, Michigan, operates nine educational centers in the Midwest. It is dedicated to helping troubled children, youth, and families find hope, security, and direction in life. All six hundred employees, from cook and janitor to president and board of trustees, have become engaged in the racial healing process. According to President Arlin Ness, the experience has had a profound impact on him and on the institution he serves:

> As a CEO and president of a large multi-service child care organization, I didn't realize how much more effective our system would have been had I dealt forthrightly with the disease of racism earlier in my life. I'm sure I could have done a much better job. However, once I became aware of the insidious effect of racism on me as an individual as well as others like me, I began to understand the tremendous effect this disease has on the culture of educational systems, businesses and

governmental agencies. This new awareness was not just an overnight experience which one picks up in watching a movie, reading a magazine or a book or having a conversation with another person, even a very wise person; but rather, it was a journey that continues today through the participation in the Institutes for the Healing of Racism. It has helped me to transform my life and thereby create a powerful harmonious working environment in Starr Commonwealth's nine centers in Michigan and Ohio. I must admit that this transformation I have experienced has been an extremely emotional one as well as a great learning experience. Becoming honest with oneself, especially about an issue like race, is not an easy undertaking. I have learned that addressing racism requires more than an intellectual commitment, it requires a mighty emotional one as well. Like others in my administrative team, I had to begin to understand what it means to have white privilege, to not have to get up in the morning and know that there are others who will look down upon me because of my skin color or ethnicity.

Because of our involvement in the Institutes for the Healing of Racism, Starr Commonwealth is on a journey to learn how to effectively implement programs that address racism in its policies affecting employees and in its treatment of programs relating to the children and families it serves daily. Our organizational environment is changing. There is a great expression of respect and affirmation of our co-workers irrespective of skin-color. Employees as well as young people are being listened to in a different way. Staff are beginning to hear what is really behind the words uttered by their colleagues as well as the young people they serve. While they recognize that the disease of racism affects white people differently than people of color, they know they are all affected by it and are committed to healing themselves. This is creating a new knowledge base for creating a safe working environment that's unlocking the potential of many individuals which I had not witnessed before. It is interesting that by becoming involved in the racial healing process, we are becoming more sensitive to other prejudices that are deeply entrenched in our national culture. And I sense in myself a desire to deal with those issues as well.

How did the marriage between Starr Commonwealth and the Institutes for the Healing of Racism come about? Several members of Starr Commonwealth's management team heard Nathan Rutstein speak at a luncheon in Marshall, Michigan. After reading his book *Healing Racism in America*, they contacted him to ask him to present a workshop for the administrators in their system. It was not long before Nathan and Reggie Newkirk were asked to do two-day workshops—as many is it would take to ensure that everyone associated with Starr Commonwealth began the racial healing process. It took more than a year to accomplish that goal.

Because service to humankind is the primary driving force at Starr Commonwealth, making such a commitment didn't require a sudden change of heart on the part of the management team. The effort required to free the institution of racial prejudice seemed only just and natural. When Arlin Ness openly acknowledged that he needed help, others came forth asking for help as well.

But not everyone in the company appreciated the institutional directive making attendance at the workshop mandatory, especially since management had the reputation of being less than heavy-handed in its dealings with employees. Though management was unaccustomed to issuing such orders, they stood firm. If a person reported ill when it was time to attend the workshop, he or she was scheduled to attend the next one that was available. Some of the cooks, gardeners, and security people wondered why they had to participate, reasoning that they had little interaction with the students. Some who worked in a counseling capacity—college-educated men and women—bristled at the idea of being told they must attend. Others—both African Americans and Whites—felt it would be a waste of time to attend because they believed nothing could change the racial conditioning of America. They had been to numerous diversity workshops, which had turned out to be exercises in futility that actually hardened participants' hidden racial views. The usually contented atmosphere at Starr Commonwealth was disrupted by a growing buzz of discontent. While the management team had taken a bold step, there was some concern among its members about what would happen if the Institutes for the Healing of Racism failed to take root within the company. James Cunningham, the Director of Training, was one of the skeptics:

> For me the healing of racism process has been both a difficult and rewarding process. Initially, I did not want to engage in another process regarding this toxic issue. Prior to beginning this experience I believed that these types of processes did nothing except promote more confusion and resentment. I entered the process guarded and angry. However, as we progressed through the two-day session and the ten cluster meetings I began to know and "feel" that this process was different. By the end of the first two-day session I had made a decision that I was going to take responsibility for healing myself and my white brothers and sisters. I began to realize that I could not heal and/or save myself without attempting to save my brothers and sisters.

I can remember that at the start I had a very physical response to approaching and groping these issues. My physical stress around the issue of racism manifested itself in pain around and about my shoulder. As I began my journey toward healing, this pain decreased and eventually disappeared.

This process with its emphasis on understanding as opposed to blaming has been very helpful to me not just in the area of issues around racism, but in dealing with people in general in a more loving and humane manner.

After undergoing the transformation process involved in the Institutes for the Healing of Racism, most of those who had balked at attending openly proclaimed that the experience was life-changing and thanked management for forcing them to participate. Today African Americans and Whites at Starr Commonwealth have real relationships with one another. There is no longer the need to pretend that everything is okay racially. Genuine caring has replaced tolerance in staff members' interactions. Friendships have developed among people who had never dreamed of getting close to someone who was so "different" from themselves. Most are making headway in internalizing the principle of the oneness of humankind. Participating in a two-day workshop has become an integral part of every new employee's job orientation.

Morale, which was always good at all nine centers, has improved considerably, attaining an unprecedented level of harmony and service-mindedness. In fact, morale has become so high that a collective urge to share the bounty with people outside of Starr Commonwealth has swept over the organization. As Arlin Ness pointed out, "We couldn't keep this to ourselves. The transformation that has taken place at Starr Commonwealth can take place in the towns where we live. And Lord knows, they—like all of us—need it."

Before long, community leaders in Calhoun County, Michigan, in which Albion is located, were approached. A series of two-day workshops was arranged for them. Close to nine hundred men and women underwent the transformational experience. Police chiefs and their deputies, foundation executives, bank presidents, college presidents and professors, fire chiefs, school principals and superintendents, corporate CEOs and vice presidents, various clergy, judges and attorneys, district prosecutors, physicians, psychologists, social workers, public health officials and heads of human service organizations, and newspaper editors and reporters participated in the workshops.

Because the response to the two-day workshops was overwhelmingly positive, the healing process was continued. The participants were grouped into clusters of ten to fifteen men and women who had gone through the same workshop together. Cluster dialogues were held once a week for ten weeks. Like the two-day workshops, the cluster groups continued the education of the mind and heart. Presentations were made about different aspects of the oneness of humankind, the origins of racism in our country, and the pathology of racism and how it affects us. The dialogue of the spirit was employed in the education-of-the-heart phase. Many of the clusters, which were formed in early 1998, are still functioning today.

There has been across-the-board praise of the experience throughout Calhoun County. The following statements from participants offer a sampling of the feedback the experience has elicited:

If I could use one word to describe my experience it would be—enlightening. It opened my eyes further to things I had been taught as a youngster that were incorrect and insensitive to those who come from a different background than me. I enjoyed learning about the experiences that my brothers and sisters of all races have had. I also gained a great deal of courage to confront issues of race and prejudices in my own family and community.

* * *

The healing of racism conference and continuing process has affected my life in a profound way. I now have a deeper sense of awareness and hope regarding racism issues.

As a young Caucasian woman I have been blinded to some of the harsh realities of racism in this world. Now that I have become more aware, I know that I play a large part in helping to heal the disease and to open the eyes of others.

As a new mother, I am now more than ever, aware that the values, beliefs, and morals that I instill into my child will make an impact in getting people to embrace the reality of the oneness of humankind.

* * *

These healing racism seminars give me hope, allow me to acknowledge myself, my history (which did not begin in the hull of a ship on its way to the "new world") and hopefully will close the gap between all of my brothers and sisters of all hues.

* * *

I was given the book *Healing Racism in America,* by Nathan Rutstein, and told to read it prior to attending the workshop. Reluctantly I read it and everything started to change from that point. First I kept turning the book over looking at the picture of the author in disbelief that this white male could be so right on. Second, I couldn't believe that our company president had ordered all of the company's employees and administrative staff to read this type of book (subsequently, all staff members had to attend the workshops).

I became so emotional during the first session that I had to excuse myself from the room for a short time. I later explained that my reaction to Nathan delivering his message about the disease of racism and its wounds felt like the Cavalry had come to my rescue to help me deliver the message that I had gotten sick and tired of delivering myself. I had become secretly angry and fed up with well-meaning racist whites who did not have a clue about the pain the race issue has caused me and people like me.

* * *

This healing racism process and the message of the oneness of humankind has helped me to medicate my wounds. Now I understand that those well-meaning whites who used to piss me off are affected by the disease of racism, and, like me, they need healing too.

* * *

As a policeman my experience with the Institute for the Healing of

Racism went through several stages. At first I was extremely guarded. I felt like every one, with the exception of my two fellow officers, were antagonistic toward me. I really didn't want to go back the second day. But I'm glad I did, because the experience opened me up to the root causes of the pain Blacks must endure every minute of their lives because of their skin color. I have grown more empathetic and understanding of their struggle to make it in a society where race prejudice is so dominant.

* * *

A police Lieutenant said,

Participating in the workshop had a profound effect on my life. Now with my African-American friends, the people I work with, we talk and they all have these painful stories to tell. You become aware of their feelings and their sensitivities and their frustrations. Participating in the workshop also increased my sensitivity to the discomfort some blacks might feel when they have to find their way through the police station to file a report or see an officer.

* * *

The editor of the largest daily newspaper in the county participated in one of the workshops and wrote in a column:

There are so many elements to Rutstein's message, that it's impossible for me to convey the depth of it in this one column. But what I could convey is the deep-in-the-heart hope it gave seminar participants. Hope that there is a way to cure the disease of racism—one that's much more effective than the traditional "fixes," such as multicultural programs and affirmative action policies.

One of the positive results from this countywide initiative was the creation of a plan to establish a center that will help educators learn to reach and teach students of color more effectively. This unprecedented endeavor is motivated by a desire to stop the psychological crippling and murder of African-American, Hispanic, and American Indian children that is taking place in many of our schools today. The center will also create curricula for elementary, middle-school, and high-school students for courses on the oneness of humankind. Teachers will receive training in how to teach the subject. Driving this initiative is the belief that the internalization of the reality of the oneness of humankind is a vaccine against the disease of racism. Helping schools to set up Institutes for the Healing of Racism on their campuses will be another function of the center. Most of the superintendents of schools in Calhoun County have endorsed the center's establishment.

News of the success in Calhoun County has spread to neighboring counties. For example, in the city of Jackson, the city administration asked Starr Commonwealth to hold a yearlong series of two-day workshops for the educational, governmental, legal, human service, journalism, and health professionals in the community. A number of administrators at a large prison in the area were so taken by the experience that they have started an Institute for the Healing of Racism for all employees and are lobbying for the head of the state prison system to establish an Institute in every Michigan prison. A number of other cities and towns have asked Starr Commonwealth to help them become involved in the racial healing process.

Starr Commonwealth's executive vice president, Marty Mitchell, who was the first in his organization to hear about the Institutes for the Healing of Racism, is amazed at what has been accomplished in such a short period of time. Based on his experience with the Institutes, he now feels optimistic that racism can be overcome:

Through my experiences in the Institute for the Healing of Racism, I have come to the realization that abuse of power, acts of superiority, and dehumanization are among the greatest threats we face as humanity. The devastating disease of racism separates us as human beings, and the only cure is to heal as one family. Having experienced the healing process, I have great hope for the future despite the many dehumanizing events that are etched into my consciousness everyday.

Because of Starr Commonwealth's success in establishing and operating Institutes for the Healing of Racism, it was only logical for the company to begin working with other organizations in Calhoun County to spearhead the creation of a national center for the healing of racism. The Kellogg Corporation, the Kellogg Foundation, and State Farm Insurance have contributed funds to set up such an entity.

Part 3

THE NATIONAL RESOURCE CENTER FOR THE HEALING OF RACISM

The primary purpose of the National Resource Center for the Healing of Racism is to provide guidance and resources that support the functioning of the Institutes for the Healing of Racism. Those who request guidance will not be under any obligation to use it. The Center will have no authority, only the responsibility to serve and help Institutes everywhere achieve their objectives and mature. The Center will encourage, inspire, and try to provide wise counsel to Institutes for the Healing of Racism that seek its help.

The guidance will come from individuals connected with the National Resource Center who have played a significant role in developing carefully evaluated Institutes for the Healing of Racism that are experiencing positive results. Those who dispense the advice will be fully aware that recipients who request their advice are free to accept or reject it as they wish.

Guidance will also come from research efforts initiated by the National Resource Center as well as from outside institutions associated with the

Center. A quarterly newsletter will keep Institutes for the Healing of Racism abreast of the latest research findings and will inform them of innovations employed by effective Institutes. To enhance the Center's research efforts, a working relationship with a regional university will be developed. Some research projects will be assigned to universities outside of Michigan. (Some faculty at Harvard have already expressed interest in working with the Center.) In time, the center will publish a journal featuring articles on research and development efforts.

To prevent rigidity from developing within the Institutes for the Healing of Racism, special task forces will be formed to work at refining their philosophy, psychology, and format. The Center will share information about new techniques and methods with all of the steering committees in North America and elsewhere. Workshops will be made available to train those who wish to implement the new techniques and methods.

A library of books, periodicals, scholarly papers, and audiotapes and videocassettes on every conceivable aspect of the issue of racism will be established. In time the library will be made available to the residents and educational institutions of Calhoun County. Monthly lectures for the public will be given at the library on topics related to the mandate of the Institutes for the Healing of Racism. The library will, from time to time, organize a series of talks by eminent scholars and activists in the field of race relations.

An audiovisual production unit will produce materials about various aspects of the philosophy, psychology, and format of the Institutes for the Healing of Racism. Materials on different aspects of the reality of the oneness of humankind, the pathology of racism, the history of racism, and other related subjects will also be produced. These materials will be marketed to institutions and individuals involved in trying to overcome racism and fostering racial unity.

The National Resource Center will also have a publishing arm that will produce books and other printed materials to aid those who are trying to overcome racism and create a harmonious society. For example, history textbooks that tell the real story of how racism was started and of how it has been maintained and promulgated in America will be produced. A concerted effort will be made to encourage schools throughout North America to use these books. A book citing the scientific and spiritual proofs of the oneness of humankind will be produced. Manuals on different aspects of the Institutes for the Healing of Racism will be published, as well as booklets about how to teach the oneness of humankind in schools, colleges, churches, synagogues, and mosques.

A department for training facilitators of Institutes will be maintained. Training sessions will be offered at the National Resource Center as well as in other locations. Trainers will also be equipped to help institutions set up Institutes for the Healing of Racism in the workplace, in schools and various governmental agencies, and in other places where people are sincerely interested in creating a healthier social climate.

The Center will organize and maintain a speakers bureau. The aims of the speakers bureau will be several: to motivate individuals and institutions to engage in the racial healing process; to assure the public that racism can indeed be overcome; to enlighten people about how racism came about in their country; to define and describe the pathology of the disease of racism and how it affects people of all skin colors; and to replace people's fractured view of the structure of humanity with a clear understanding of the realities underlying the principle of the oneness of humankind.

ιter will organize an annual international conference that will be open to all members of the Institutes for the Healing of Racism and their friends. The conference will feature speakers who will share information intended to help improve attendees' effectiveness as racial healing practitioners. Workshops will be held to demonstrate how new techniques and methods can be applied. There will be a panel discussion featuring the success stories of a variety of Institutes from different regions of the world. A special time will be set aside for people to exchange experiences. Another period will be devoted to giving attendees an opportunity to offer recommendations on how to improve the operations of the Institutes for the Healing of Racism. Programs will be organized to foster a sense of familyhood. Entertainment at the conference will reflect the principles of oneness and unity in diversity.

Throughout the year the Center will sponsor seminars for different constituencies. For example, leading business people, health professionals, or law enforcement officials will be brought together to discuss various aspects of the racial condition in their work communities. The primary objective of this enterprise will be to inspire and encourage participants to start Institutes within their organizations.

To encourage youth to become involved in fostering racial harmony in their communities, the National Resource Center will promote the concept of race unity workshops. The Center will encourage local high schools to offer workshops for credit and will offer personal and material guidance on how to set up the workshops.

The Center will encourage college students to organize race unity workshops. It will also encourage college administrators and faculty to establish six-credit courses on the Institutes for the Healing of Racism. During the first semester, students will learn how to participate in and facilitate a dialogue session. Besides learning how to listen with the heart, students will take part in an interdisciplinary educational experience. They will be given biological, genetic, anthropological, historical, sociological, and psychological information. During the second semester they will participate in a community service project. Groups of three or four students will go into the community at large to set up Institutes for the Healing of Racism in youth centers, schools, churches, synagogues, Head-Start programs, youth correctional institutions, and other places.

The Center's public information office will keep local, regional, and national news media up to date with newsworthy activities of the Institutes for the Healing of Racism. The Center will function as a national voice for local initiatives that are of national interest. For example, the work that the Institutes in Grand Rapids, Michigan, are doing; or what the Institutes' four hundred members are doing in Anchorage, Alaska. The Public Information Office (PIO) will run an annual workshop for Institutes PIO representatives on how to interact with the news media, how to write news releases, and how to determine which events may be newsworthy.

An active Web site will be established.

The Center will produce a newsletter that will be both inspirational and educational for all of the members of the Institutes for the Healing of Racism in North America and elsewhere. The newsletter will highlight what some of the most successful Institutes are doing and how they went about doing it. It will also feature an editorial page that will feature members' testimonials about what their involvement in the Institutes for the Healing of Racism has meant to them. Profiles of noteworthy individuals involved in the Institutes will be included.

Once the National Resource Center is firmly established, it will network with likeminded organizations such as the Southern Poverty Law Center and the Conflict Management Group. It will also seek Non-Governmental Organization (NGO) status with the United Nations.

Though the Center will be a nonprofit entity, it will seek and administer funds to keep its operations functioning smoothly. Grants from foundations and governmental agencies will be sought. Monies will be derived from its publications, audiovisual enterprises, its speakers bureau, and its training endeavors.

THE FUTURE OF THE INSTITUTES FOR THE HEALING OF RACISM

While scores of Institutes for the Healing of Racism have sprung up in North America, Europe, and Australia, there has been no attempt—nor even a remote desire—to become the dominant force in wiping out the disease of racism in the world. The Institutes' primary focus is to serve individuals and institutions by helping them to heal their racism. Our belief is that by doing so communities will eventually unite in a genuine effort to internalize the reality of the oneness of humankind. Wherever that happens, we will draw closer to realizing the ancient dream of uniting the human family.

We suffer from no illusions that ours is the only way to eradicate racism. We persist in our efforts because we witness people benefiting from them day after day. Should that someday stop, the Institutes for the Healing of Racism would cease operations. Recognizing that other organizations are also experiencing significant success in overcoming racism, we try to network with them, for we believe that obtaining credit for what we are doing is not as important as working in a truly united fashion with other likeminded groups to eliminate scourge of racism.

Those who serve selflessly and are motivated by a genuine desire to help their fellow human beings are the most successful practitioners in the racial healing process. When an individual or group of individuals tries to use the Institutes to promote themselves or their particular ideologies, they usually fail.

We have noticed over the years that some Institutes succeed while others fail. What leads to success? We have observed that the following factors are part of the pattern of success:

1. The great majority of participants are genuinely committed to healing themselves and others of the disease of racism.
2. They understand the nature of racism.
3. They are persistent and patient.
4. They put the cause ahead of the need for notoriety or social or political status.
5. They have a fairly clear view of what they want to achieve and a working understanding of how to implement that vision.
6. They adopt the attitude of a selfless and humble crusader.
7. They are conscious of the principle of the oneness of humankind and earnestly strive to internalize it, becoming, as a result, a force for unity in their community.

What of the future of the Institutes for the Healing of Racism? It is not something to which we devote much time, energy, or thought. We believe that doing so would detract from our primary mission, which is to heal the disease of racism and promote unity in our communities.

While we do not keep count of how many Institutes exist, we are none-theless engaged in a process of growth. The principle that guides our growth is one that the Christophers, a Catholic order, tries to live by: "Instead of cursing the darkness, light a candle."

Whenever an Institute becomes well grounded, it develops a natural urge to help an institution—public or private—establish its own Institute for the Healing of Racism. The motive is to share with others what is helping us. To do so is comparable to lighting a candle in the community at large. Should most of the community's institutions begin to operate flourishing Institutes, that community becomes racially enlightened.

Some communities in North America and Britain are making significant headway toward racial enlightenment. Grand Rapids, Michigan, tradition-ally a conservative city, serves as a case in point.

In 1994, a socially enlightened CEO named Robert Woodrick read the book *Healing Racism in America: A Prescription for the Disease* and invited author Nathan Rutstein to Grand Rapids to help set up an Institute for his management team. Woodrick didn't let Nathan go home until he had de-scribed the philosophy and psychology of the Institutes for the Healing of Racism to city leaders. The corporate executive was using Nathan to plant some seeds.

After a second visit from Nathan, Woodrick was on his own.

Today most of the seeds that Woodrick planted have flowered. There are now full-time Institutes for the Healing of Racism and scores of clusters associated with each Institute in Grand Rapids: the Bar Association; the Chamber of Commerce; every high school; every college; most of the Ro-man Catholic and Episcopalian churches; some Dutch Reformed churches; eleven corporations, including Steel Case Inc., which employs more than fifteen thousand men and women; Rotary International; and the police department. A special training program for corporate executives has been set up by the Grand Rapids Chamber of Commerce. The success of the Chamber's efforts is evidenced by a waiting list of workshop candidates that often numbers some two hundred or more people from area businesses and industry. There are more than thirty trained facilitators, some of whom provide facilitating training programs for newly established Institutes in neighboring cities. Muskegon, one of those cities, has caught the Grand Rapids spirit and now has forty racial healing programs of its own operating within a number of diverse institutions. Every new teacher hired by the Muskegon public school system must go through an Institute healing program. In fact, the superintendent of schools has made it a goal to establish an Institute in every one of the city's schools.

Those who are guiding the development of the Institutes for the Healing of Racism in Grand Rapids have been able to measure scientifically its impact on the city. A 1998 study by an independent research organization showed that 98 percent of Institute participants rated their experience "very good" or better, and 61 percent rated their experience "excellent." Participants overwhelmingly agreed that racism is a significant social issue that affects everybody—for a 5.9-point "total agreement" score on a 6-point scale. The vast majority of respondents reported they are motivated to heal racism in their personal and work lives as a result of their Institute experience, and they want to "stand out" as advocates of racial healing. Both minorities and Whites said that they have become more aware of racism in their own lives and called the Institute experience "worthwhile," "powerful," "moving," or "educational." A few Institute participants used adjectives such as "confusing" or "political" to describe their experience, but the overall results of the study were extremely positive. Ninety-three percent said they would "most likely" recommend the Institute experience to others.

Because of the efforts of the Institutes for the Healing of Racism in Grand Rapids, the editor of the local African-American weekly newspaper declared, "For the first time Blacks in this city have hope."

A White executive who has undergone the special training offered by the Grand Rapids Chamber of Commerce explains what she has gained from her experience with the Institutes for the Healing of Racism:

To hear the revelations from my friends and colleagues of color about their innermost feelings based on the racism that they experience each and every day of their lives made me angry and frustrated!

As one of the African-American participants said to the group, "Wake up white people, you have been lied to and have been sedated into thinking that things are better."

Well, I am awake and now more aware than ever before! The persons of color in the group are to be commended for repeating time and time again their stories. It is an emotional and gut-wrenching experience and I am eternally grateful that I was given the opportunity to wake up! Thank you so much.

APPENDIX
THE DIALOGUE FORMAT

	Purpose	Tips for Facilitating
Welcoming Remarks, Introductions: (10 minutes)	To welcome everyone and to begin the process of truly seeing each other.	• Facilitators should welcome everyone, briefly state the reason for gathering and the goals of the Institute, and then have everyone introduce themselves. • If time permits, facilitators may invite participants to share what strengths each of them brings to the gathering and what they hope to get out of it. • At subsequent meetings, when participants are acquainted with one another, facilitators may ask if anyone wishes to share thoughts or experiences since the last meeting. • A sign-in book should also be kept with a running list of each week's participants. Facilitators should remind everyone to sign it before they leave if they did not sign it upon entering. • Any announcements should be made before beginning the presentation.
Presentation: (20–30 minutes)	The Institutes for the Healing of Racism aim to educate the heart and the mind. This specific segment is directed at the mind. It is designed to disseminate information that is helpful to understanding the oneness of humankind and the history and pathology of racism in our communities and in our nation. This segment of the dialogue focuses on factual information.	• Copies of the presentation materials (articles, overhead transparencies, summary of movies shown, outlines of lectures, etc.) should be distributed to participants either before or after the actual presentation so they can compile a notebook of references. • Try to plan presentations as far ahead of time as possible. At the beginning of each course or meeting series, map out a tentative progression of topics you would like to see addressed, and generate a list of possible presenters/presentations. • Vary the medium of presentation from week to week (video, lecture, activity, etc.).

	Purpose	Tips for Facilitating
Presentation (con't): (20–30 minutes)		• Be sure to ask presenters as soon as possible if they will need any special equipment (TV/VCR, overhead projector, flip chart, etc.).
Question/Meditation: (5 minutes)	The question that the rest of the dialogue will center on is intended to make participants aware of their own experiences and feelings in relation to a specific topic. The main purpose is to help participants become acquainted with their true racial conditioning.	• Facilitators should tell the participants that they are going to pose a question and ask them to meditate on the question. • The question should be repeated twice, slowly. Participants are instructed to close their eyes while the question is asked a second time. • In silence, everyone meditates on the question for 4 minutes. • The question should be well thought out ahead of time so as to really encourage people to extrapolate their responses from personal experiences and feelings. It should guide them into sharing their feelings and making them look inward for a response rather than to knowledge of external events.
Pairing Off: (10 minutes)	This is an important part of the dialogue. It is designed to foster effective listening skills and deep listening. This allows people to feel comfortable sharing their personal stories and also allows each person to feel truly seen and heard; it is a validating experience to have one's feelings taken this seriously. This validation gives people the courage to acknowledge and treat the disease of racism. As a result of this process, each participant feels as if	• Partner A responds to the question while Partner B listens, never uttering a word, using nonverbal communication to show support and entirely withholding judgment or evaluation. (4 minutes) • After 4 minutes, one of the facilitators walks around to each pair and asks them to switch (B responds while A listens). • It should be decided ahead of time which of the facilitators will do this. At the beginning of each session, it should be determined whether there is an odd or even number of participants. If odd, the predetermined "timer" should sit out. It should not

	Purpose	Tips for Facilitating
Pairing Off (con't): (10 minutes)	they have at least one ally when they go back to share with the group.	be the same person each week; facilitators should alternate. • After another 4 minutes the "timer" goes around and asks participants to come back together.
Group Dialogue: (30–45 minutes)	This is a time for human transformation. The same listening skills that were exercised in one-on-one sharing are practiced here as participants in the group share the feelings and experiences the question evoked in them. This is not a time to give each other advice. As participants share their struggles with the disease of racism, each person gains a deeper understanding of its pathology.	• Once all of the participants have returned to the circle, one of the facilitators welcomes everyone back and announces that it is time to share with the entire group. • At this point the Guidelines for Sharing are read aloud. One of the facilitators reads them all slowly, or the guidelines are passed around and each participant reads one and then counts to 5 before passing them on. • After the guidelines are read, the question is repeated, and participants are invited to share.

Closing:
(10–15 minutes)
	It is important to leave people feeling empowered to change rather than feeling depressed. A closing exercise should emphasize that this is only a beginning. It should encourage participants to seek other resources and continue working on the issues raised during the sharing.	• After 30–45 minutes of sharing, tell participants that it is time to close, and if time permits ask if anyone else needs to share before the meeting is closed.
		• Initiate a closure that involves everyone. One possibility is to have everyone go around and answer a closing question before the actual closing circle is initiated. This is intended to engage everyone with the exception of anyone who explicitly states the desire to pass on the question. Some possible questions:
		   - What have you learned today?
		   - What have you thought about in a new way today?
		   - What concerns have challenged you? Can we brainstorm about potential things to do?

Purpose	Tips for Facilitating
Closing (con't): (10–15 minutes)	- How can we stay in touch to discuss future developments involving the diverse issue we explored today? • To officially close the meeting, have everyone stand and hold hands in a meditative circle for a few minutes. It is important to remember that the intent is to create a spiritual space, an exchange of energy to carry participants forward. Comments at this time should be short and positive. This is not a time to clarify earlier comments, give advice that has been held back, or apologize for any perceived faults. It is a time to express gratitude or inspiration. Anyone who is moved to share a thought is welcome to do so, while it is also entirely appropriate if everyone remains silent for the entire duration.